DUMBELL

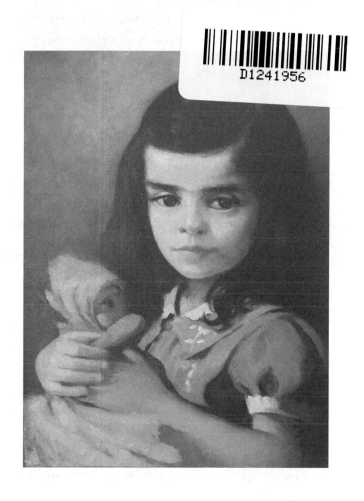

Marian Christy

2020 White Bird
www.whitebirdpublications.com

Published in the United States by
White Bird Publication, LLC, Texas

ISBN 978-1-63363-459-6
eBook ISBN 978-1-63363-460-2
Library of Congress Control Number 2020930109

Cover design: E. Kusch
Cover picture taken by Kathleen Flett

Printed in the United States of America

Dedication

In remembrance of my late mother, Anna Christy, a great beauty who was spiritually superior and my earthly guide.

Special thanks to my visionary publisher and editor, Evelyn M. Byrne-Kusch, one of my 1,000 angels, and a woman of great wisdom.

Acknowledgement

Her name was Anna.

She loved sunshine days, expanses of green grass mowed to perfection, all living flowers and, most of all, me.

When I left the little house we shared, when I left her side, to cover European haute couture for my newspaper, she wrote to me every day in perfect oversized penmanship. Anna's daily missals followed me on long assignments to Rome-Paris-Madrid-Athens-London-Dublin—everywhere.

I cherish those '60s-'70s letters.

The ink is faded, but the wonderful words are still readable. The tissue paper on which Anna wrote on has become crinkly. It rustles. Anna rustled when she was close by. I think she still is around. And when I read again, and still again, her words of pride, pure joy, that I'd accomplished so much with so little, I can hear her lilting voice of encouragement. That forever voice is tucked into worn air mail envelopes with old stamps. Those letters sustain me when my world gets cloudy, when a storm is brewing on the horizon.

My real mother's name was Anna Christy. She bears no resemblance to the confused-bullied Mommy in this book except on three important counts: she was a gorgeous woman, a gifted fashion designer and an extraordinary crochet artisan.

Anna was also an outspoken critic of all things imperfect, like a hair out of place or a too-flashy lipstick. "What difference does it make?" When I asked her that question she answered hesitatingly: "Because… because I want you to be perfect."

That's just the thing. Perfection was never included in the human condition.

What she meant and, oh yes, my mother did speak in shorthand, is that perfection is an unattainable goal but, in making the stretch, you can closer to becoming better than you think you are. She never wanted me to think I was down and out, only down. "And that's temporary," she assured me.

She believed in miracles, undue generosity, never giving up, in self-improvement, in having faith that defies reason. She inspired this book about beating the odds, especially bullying. It is dedicated to her memory. It is meant to reflect her philosophy that anyone caught in a terrible snare, like bullying, is fully capable of redemption.

The truth of me is that Anna not only birthed me, she birthed my journalism career. No one ever achieves anything of significance alone.

She was the force who stood on the sidelines applauding my primitive beginnings in journalism, my $10 a story start. Ten dollars meant a lot to us then. In one letter she makes a serious confession. She was so happy to see my byline on Page One that she *dared* to spend $10 on getting her hair done at the tiny neighborhood salon down the street. She made it sound like that $10 fling was a celebration of me, that what one of us achieved effected the other. We were a team, a mother-daughter duo who appeared to be sisters.

When I was able to buy her a new red car, a lovely mink jacket with a matching beret, cancer ate her alive.

This book is in her honor because she was on the sidelines when jealous competitors tried to smear me, when people I thought were friends fell into the Judas category, when a promotion within my newspaper made envious colleagues double crossers.

She was always on the sidelines quoting from herself.

"God is with you so who can hurt you?" Or: "Never second guess yourself. Stick to your intuition." Or: her everlasting cheer when she shared a glass of wine together: "To your heart's desire." She was always blessing me. She told me not to regret her final absence, that there would always be angels around to protect me. This was one of the last things she told me in the hospital, just before she died, when she could still speak. I was so bitter as I watched her disappear through death's door that I couldn't cry.

Angels?

I reminded myself that my mother was on morphine.

Years later, I don't know how many, I met a fine woman, Kathleen Flett, by chance, at a Boston Museum of Fine Arts dinner. Her teenage daughter, Katie, a budding artist, had died suddenly in a fatal car crash and, did I know, that angels were a main source of solace and... I thought this poor woman, this stranger, is hallucinating.

Over the years we became friends, and over the same years, Kathleen took course after course on "Angels," their untapped power and their everlasting glory. I listened with interest but not faith. Kathleen never gave up on me. She told me endless angel stories, believable ones, and I began to consider angel potentiality. Once, when I struggled with a walker, when I was intractable, she watched me bend down, *on my own,* to pick up a shiny new penny on the sidewalk. "Angels," she confirmed with unbridled certainty.

I made a wish on that penny. It was that this book come to fruition.

One terrible day, on my own, I had to go into surgery for the serious stuff. I was signing in, sober, street clothes still on, when I asked the receptionist his name? "Angelo," he said. I was nervous and had missed his name tag. When I was put on the gurney, I looked at the sheet. It had "Angelica," Latin for angel, written all over it. It was Christmas time. When I was wheeled into the operating room, I heard someone singing the lyrics from "Hark the Herald Angels Sing." I fell asleep surrounded by angels, 1,000 of them.

These are the guideposts that lit the idea for this book.

I hope you discover in it something wonderful, some small golden nugget, that you can make take and make your own.

DUMBELL

**White Bird
Publications**

Prologue

I am now in my eighth decade. The longitude and latitude of the actual year no longer matter.

I am in the lowest level of the hospital, completing a trying day of pre-op interrogations and physical tests that precede a total knee replacement.

I hobble. A cane is my companion. Cortisone has lost its witchcraft.

The orthopedic surgeon's final words were ominous. If I fall again, I will, most likely, break a hip, or worse. *The wheelchair existence awaits you,* he warned.

His nonchalant advice was for me to go right to Admissions and fill out the reams of paperwork connected to the surgery.

The final hospital questioner, a sour woman wearing everything blood red, including a hasty slash of lipstick that matched her funky ballet shoes, declared the day's medical rigmarole was nearly complete.

Just one more question.

"Have you ever been emotionally abused?"

I was shocked into disbelief. "What connects a knee replacement to, to…"

I could not utter the words "emotionally abused."

The woman in red interrupted the terrible trauma gripping me.

She told me that the "emotional abuse" question was now a standard inquiry before all major surgeries. What? She was in a hurry. She had no time for the earthquake exploding inside me. She quickly checked off the "no" box.

That was a mistake, a lie.

I belonged in the "yes" box. I am boxed there forever. One out of eight children are bullied at home.

I am one of them and I remember everything.

Chapter One
Acting Up

Sometimes I pretended to be deaf.

I hated it when I overheard Mommy's terrified gasps, no words, just gasps. Daddy was threatening to take me, steal me, have me kidnapped, and she'd never see me, her firstborn, again.

I was terrified of the parental war blasting away.

I hated being the target.

Slammed doors followed Daddy's bullying.

Daddy, who'd been an amateur wrestler, darted out of the front door.

His slam sounded like a lion's roar. Mommy sped to their cramped bedroom, so close to the sidewalk, so convenient for gossipy eavesdroppers, that it was embarrassing. Bang! Mommy's slam sounded like the perfect clichéd message of intense anger: do not disturb under any circumstance.

The sounds of slammed doors at each end of the house,

doors slammed at each other, one after the other, always seemed to concern me in some mysterious way.

I didn't understand the seed of this chaos or that it seemed to involve me.

Daddy had a sinister mightiness about him. He demanded my silence at all times. I didn't speak because I was petrified to speak. I did as I was told. I was a terrified little girl, barely ten years old, and embroiled in a painful family quandary over which I had no control. That's how I became meek, and passive, and malleable.

But I was also impressionable. My memory never failed me. I seemed to have a forever recorder buried in my soul. It absorbed everything.

When I replayed my memories, I always pondered the "why" of my high-intensity situation.

Why, and how, could I be the cause of such a horrid house war?

Why was I the source of this nasty conflict, this noisy and contentious battle that the neighbors could hear so clearly? Why did Mommy internalize her emotional battering with a cool detachment that I found appalling?

The truth is that I always tried to shut out, shut up, the fractures of emotional abuse.

That's why I played deaf.

Of course, I followed Daddy's irrevocable patriarchal rule of silence. Daddy was capable of doing Mommy and me great physical harm. He was built like a bear. Maybe that's why Mommy kept to herself. She gave Daddy no provocation to get violent.

When he rumbled past me, yelling that I, a little girl, had household duties, I liked it better when he stomped by me as if I were invisible. Mommy, who used to love singing and accompanying herself on the piano, slid the cover over the keyboard solemnly. I knew that the music in her had died.

Mommy became a serious stoic, a great beauty who, behind closed doors, stifled her cries into a pillow. She thought I wouldn't hear her sounds of sorrow. Having a useless tongue, my ears and eyes became like sponges that absorbed everything, even peripheral sounds and sights. I heard Mommy's cries. I felt their shrill pierce.

I played deaf because I didn't want to acknowledge that I was, somehow, the focus of these awful ruckuses. When I didn't want to hear something, I acted as if I were distracted. I concentrated on something else, something distant. I let my eyes go blank. I showed no reactions. I was acting.

I had assumed deafness on my own. Muteness was Daddy's making. It was so easy to pretend I was a deaf-mute. I was at the center of a perfect storm.

The trouble was that I didn't know when, exactly, to turn off my ears or when to leave them on. I wasn't an efficient child. I lost control, lost good judgment about when to listen and when not to listen. I was also a foolish child playing the survival game. I tried to erect protective walls around me, invisible ones.

I forgot that real deafness could be permanent. I forgot that I was only playing. When Daddy wasn't around, I listened and reacted with words spoken to myself but never out loud. I had always loved words, speaking them, and writing them. Someday I'd be a wordsmith.

I knew if I were to indulge successfully in this deaf game, I would have to play deaf constantly. Inconsistency would spoil everything.

I had no integrity. I was becoming a phony. There were some things that I wanted to hear. I was anxious to put together the pieces of the puzzle of me. I needed to understand the reasons behind my chilling dilemma.

I got careless.

There were times I threw caution to the winds and talked a blue streak to my dog who tilted his head and raised his ears to listen hard. I told my dog everything, all the things I'm telling you now.

Be careful, I reminded myself. You could get caught in the web of your cunning little game. Daddy has bigger ears than you.

I was a nervous girl who bit her nails, used bare knuckles to claw little holes into the stucco wall leaning against her tiny bed. Once, when a compulsive yowl got stuck in my throat, I plucked out a single long eyelash with one determined pull. It felt like the sting of an inoculation needle.

Daddy noticed the multi-colored bruising.

When I slumped silently, in his shadow, he asked Mommy bluntly: "What's wrong with the dumbbell?" Mommy shrugged, eyes downcast. Daddy's glance was scrolled with disgust.

I was overwhelmed with deep-rooted insecurities. I wanted to punish myself for the plunge into the nothingness into which I'd fallen or been thrust. Where I lived emotionally was deep and dark. The ache was constant. Intense, too.

Pretending deafness was the only defense I could muster. Daddy's silence ruling clinched my scheme into something bigger.

My ears worked. I heard everything. My eyes became like a second set of ears.

And when I saw it all, and more than all, I continued to talk to myself without making a sound. Everything in my world took on an air of transparency. I was also a curious girl with a sharp mind's eye. I was always trying to figure out the whys and wherefores of the marital war exploding around me.

Mommy was always angry now.

How could I, an exemplary Miss Obedience, be the cause?

I didn't know then that Mommy's romantic frustration, a marriage gone terribly wrong, could unhinge a pretty woman. Mommy didn't smile at me. She stared. In that stare, I saw displeasure. So I closed my eyes, held a blink too long. That's when I thought about pretending to be blind too.

It never came to that.

Mommy noticed that my ears appeared to malfunction.

She dragged me to a doctor, a children's hearing specialist. *Tell me,* she said to the tall, gray-haired man wearing crisp starched whites, *is my child going deaf?*

I was fascinated by the complicated machines which had buttons that, when pressed, vibrated different sounds at different levels. I got lost in a fascinating whirl of soft sounds versus loud sounds. The hearing tests, so extraordinary, so challenging, involved a receiver clamped to one ear and then the other.

What an amusing sport this was. Fun! I didn't know that medical hearing tests could masquerade as entertainment.

The doctor smiled. He assured my mother that my hearing was excellent.

She shot me an exasperated glance.

I started biting my nails, what was left of them.

A twinge of guilt hit me.

I had become a true fake, like Daddy, but not like Daddy.

My fakery was about self-preservation. Daddy was just plain mean.

The man in white saw me damaging my nails, made brief eye contact with Mommy, and mumbled something about "selective hearing" and how it was linked to stress. He told Mommy to go to the drugstore, get a colorless nail liquid designed to burn my mouth and tongue, a reminder that bitten nails are a no-no.

I immediately played deaf again, deaf to the medicine's predicted impact. I didn't want to burn. Why did I have to burn? Burn hurt.

My ears merged the two key words, burn and bad.

I was bad. Daddy said so. Bad girls get burned.

Mommy said nothing as she yanked me toward the car and shoved me into the back seat.

Her chilly silence, forbidding, escalated into a deep

frown that wrinkled her brow. It erased her dazzling million-dollar smile. Her almond-shaped brown eyes were sparked with the accumulated anger she'd hidden inside. Now, when Daddy had his fits, her inner rage was settled on me.

Her mouth, she had beautiful lips painted red, settled into a straight hard line. Mommy was mad, very mad, at me.

I loved her beyond reason. I never guessed that Daddy had, by then, shattered her spirit, left her irate and hostile, and that's why she thought nothing of splintering my spirit so that it matched hers.

She was in a kind of jail, a locked cell, and she wanted my misery to match hers. Only a psychiatrist could explain Mommy's deep complexities and how they twisted her into a torment so desolate that it made her want to include me in her wretchedness.

All I knew was that Mommy didn't love me like before. I was no longer her dear little girl. I was her hostage. I couldn't identify the specifics of what I had done, which was absolutely nothing, to deserve her wrath. I had been relegated to silence. I couldn't even ask her where I'd gone wrong.

I was a stupid, idiotic little girl to play deaf. I forgave myself. Mommy did not forgive me. Daddy always called me a Dumbbell. He also referred to me only as "She."

I had a name. But Daddy had rendered me useless and nameless. I needed a confidante who'd never spill my awful secrets.

Who?

My doggie.

Chapter Two
My Buddy

I had one friend.

He was smaller than me, had licorice hair just like me, and his speckled amber eyes got moist when I crushed him to my heart and cried into his little body, telling him how bereft I felt and why.

We snuggled close. We blurred into one.

Teddy was a small dog—an abandoned mongrel that wandered into our ugly yard, a tiny dirt floor. I claimed him as he claimed me, instantly and unconditionally. I had fallen in love. My feelings for Teddy were mutual and addictive.

I was so hooked on Teddy that I imagined he was human, that he understood my plight. He nestled into my arms, a perfect fit. When I spoke what was in my heart to him, he didn't move a muscle. He perked his ears. He listened intently.

When you're ten years old, you don't think in terms of ulterior motives.

The very afternoon immediately following the fateful hearing test, my doggie and I were playing together. Mommy let me delay my endless chores for a few minutes. I thought she was being very nice. I thought she'd forgiven my deaf fiasco.

I also thought I still had a little gumption left, a desire to unchain myself, play with Teddy and pretend normality. A ball was involved. So was the chase. The love between Teddy and me was huge, obvious and true.

I threw. Teddy caught. We were in perfect tandem. We were a pair, like human twins. When we played, I abandoned my melancholy. I was happy. I didn't realize that Teddy had rescued me from going crazy. I didn't even know that I needed to be rescued. I never even thought I was worthy of rescue. Who would want me besides Daddy's kidnappers?

Mommy told me, many times, that Daddy had plans to have me kidnapped.

I played deaf.

Inexperienced little girls have no idea how quickly the fizz of joy can vanish, that significant emotional disasters are always imminent. I didn't know yet that Teddy taught me the power of requited love or that courage and love have a link.

I had no idea that our backyard was also a battlefield, that I'd soon be emotionally crippled, or that my pain would last a lifetime.

All I saw for real were exaggerated flashing red lights going on off, on off.

What happened next was a tyrannical lesson in emotional abuse.

It was like a movie reel in slow motion.

A workman, a stranger, pulled up in an idling flatbed farm truck and made eye contact with Mommy. He left his flashers on. He put the gear in park. Mommy nodded once from behind the kitchen's screen door.

This bald intruder, in dirty coveralls over a sleeveless undershirt wet with blotches of sweat, swooped into the yard, swept Teddy into his hairy arms, ran to his idling vehicle, and raced away.

For a split second, I was numb with shock. I was deaf no more. I heard shrieks. They seemed distant, as if the frenzied, ear-splitting bellows were coming from somewhere else, someone else. The shrill sounds were loud and clear. They exploded from me.

I screamed. I sobbed. I bawled. I hollered.

I ran after the truck fast, desperately.

The truck sped up, careened around a corner, and disappeared with Teddy inside. For a nanosecond, I stood alone on the sidewalk, emotionally exhausted. My physical energy froze too. My girlish protests were weak when compared to the horsepower of a speeding truck racing away with Teddy aboard.

Stop! Stop! Stop! I had yelled as loudly as I could yell.

Teddy! Teddy! Don't take my Teddy! Teddy!

The truck was nowhere in sight. There was no Teddy anymore. The chase was over. I was done. The man, hired and paid for by Daddy, had done Mommy's bidding. Later I heard Daddy ask her if she was pleased? I didn't want to believe what I'd just heard. I blotted it out. I played deaf again. How could cruelty bring Mommy pleasure?

I have no inkling how I staggered home, tears flowing, needing a spot to weep again, in earnest, in private, with more intensity than was possible for a little girl. I staggered into my bedroom, weak and unsteady, found the wall where I'd made holes, leaned against it, and slid to the floor. It was a slump of woe.

I was loud and convulsive.

I heard myself moaning. I was hysterical. I wasn't deaf. I didn't care who heard me. The neighbors, Mommy. Everyone. I just gave into myself.

I screeched with wild abandon. Mommy, who'd ignored her little girl having her first nervous breakdown, would later find me, still weeping final pitiful sobs, gasping for breath, curled against the wall I had vandalized, stuck in the fetal position.

I was already a damaged child, totally defeated by the one I had held dearest, my Mommy. I loved her so much. I remembered how much she'd cared for me when I was smaller. She'd curled my hair in rags. We walked hand-in-hand. We had vanilla cones together. We went to Shirley Temple movies together. We'd been togetherness itself.

Daddy changed that. When he changed Mommy, he changed everything.

I wanted Teddy back. Where was Teddy? He had loved me the way Mommy did once.

That's when I began to think love didn't exist long. It left you feeling alone, pushed you into darkness, rammed you to the sidelines, and left you unacknowledged and unwanted. Love was linked to rejection, to loss. It had inherent dangers. The price of love was colossal.

I told myself to be very, very careful about who or what I loved.

My doggie, my playmate, had been taken, kidnapped. Teddy had disappeared. I wanted to disappear too. I was incoherent with grief. Teddy had died out of my life. I would have to die to get him back. My thoughts were an illogical jumble. I wondered how I, too, could die?

Then a fleeting ray of hope, false, hit me. Maybe the man who snatched Teddy would come back and snatch me, reunite me with my doggie.

I realized, in one violent howl, that Teddy was gone forever and ever. Teddy's heartrending disappearance was swift. That's what made it so unmerciful, so cruel. Mommy planned this. When had she become a bully? When had she become like Daddy?

I slipped or was tossed somewhere deep and low. Down, down, down I went. Yes, I must be bad. Why else would Teddy be seized from me? I was bad. I deserved bad things. I began to do bad things to myself.

My black hair hung in two long braids that needed new braiding.

I'd been pulling one hard. It hurt, but not bad enough. I pulled the other even harder. It hurt more. I forced suffering on myself with every yank. I was in despair. I felt desolate. I pulled on my braids again and again, one after the other, again and still again. It hurt, burned my skull like a bolt of fire. I pulled harder. That's what I thought I deserved...burn. I was desolate, lost.

Unbearable grief gripped me. It wouldn't let go. I longed for Teddy. I wasn't rational. I was trying to pull my hair out of my scalp in a clump, the whole braid, all at once.

I wanted to harm myself physically. I was to blame for this tragic loss. I didn't know the root of it. I didn't know anything. Playing deaf was just play. My concocted self-defense mechanism had ricocheted. Mommy had chalked up my pretend deafness to sheer willfulness. That infuriated her. I was too young to fathom the depth of her wrath or how it could make her so fierce.

Slashed wrists among children were unknown then. I'd never touched Daddy's razor. The only way I thought I could hurt myself was to pull my hair out. So I pulled again and again. Hard. Hard.

My nails were already bitten beyond the quick. I was a pathetic child, and if my teeth could eat more finger skin from around the nail bed, they did. I was nauseous whenever I was in a car. I was always afraid that I was going to be dumped somewhere, discarded to kidnappers. I had headaches. I got dizzy when Daddy came home. I honored his unflinching rule of complete silence. I stayed out of his way.

I was the girl both unseen and unheard.

Thinking of Teddy, I screeched again and again. My piercing hollering became shriller. I bawled again until I was hoarse. Teddy! I wanted Teddy back! Or, better, I wanted to be wherever Teddy was now!

Eventually, I lost all track of time. Complete exhaustion made me limp, unable to move. I thought I was dying. I'd heard about angels and heaven, about being lifted somehow, somewhere high in the clouds.

Maybe I was there, with them, the angels. Maybe I'd hear them whisper a kind word in my ear, or hum a song. I thought maybe a choir of angels, 1,000 of them, would sing me their consolation. My imagination was like a salve, a soothing balm for all the venom that had been needled into me.

I saw a shadow move near me.

It was Mommy.

She looked down at me. Her eyes were full of disdain. Her first machete words slashed right through me.

"Those are crocodile tears," she accused shrewishly.

I didn't know what crocodile tears were. All I knew about crocodiles was that the ugly beasts lived in swamps and gobbled up little children eating them alive.

But I, a wounded girl shrunk to nothing by Teddy-torment, guessed what Mommy was insinuating. She was saying that my tears were an act, a performance, just like my deafness was an act, or, as she later put it, "a trick."

All I knew then was that Mommy's words, crocodile tears, ripped at an already shredded heart. Mommy didn't care about the depth of my loss. Or maybe she did. She seemed to revel in breaking me, making me her companion in gloom.

When had her fury over Daddy's totalitarianism exploded into cruelty toward me?

Mommy had mastered talking in shorthand. She could spit poison darts with bull's eye precision.

When Daddy attacked her with accusations and tirades she didn't deserve, she sputtered a stinging phrase indistinctly, under her breath. Once, she turned her back on him when he was raging and mumbled softly: "Street angel, house devil." He was so busy yelling at her, bullying her, that he didn't hear her words.

I did.

Mommy wanted me to know what she thought of Daddy.

Now, speaking to me, she hissed hateful words: "You're just like your father." She hated Daddy. I wasn't deaf to Mommy's miserable new insinuation. Comparing me to him meant she hated me too.

I hung my head in shame.

I stared at the floor.

I thought, *When had Mommy, my once-sweet Mommy, become such a spitfire? I was not anything like Daddy. At that moment, I was her prey.*

Why had I believed she didn't want me kidnapped? Why did I think she was my ally, my defender? Her voice, the dear voice that had sung hymns and hummed popular tunes, now dripped sarcasm and scorn.

"You're just like your father..."

I would never again cry with such wild abandon. Self-doubt shook me until I shivered in the heat. A dark sky stayed dark. That's the precise moment the residue of my confidence shattered into a million pieces.

Mommy seemed satisfied that she hurt me so much, and with such surprising sneakiness. It placated or soothed the storm raging within her. It was as if she was swatting at an awful personal hurt, some stumbling block caused by me, something that I never knew was my fault.

Her inner rage was unrelenting, the kind that grinds internal organs and causes diseases like cancer and Parkinson's. She ended up with both.

"You're just like your father," she repeated.

When she compared me to Daddy three times, I surrendered something golden in me: hope. I was a hopeless child. Bad. My situation was hopeless. Bad. Maybe I was going to be kidnapped after all.

I was a little girl pushed into a state of melancholy that still haunts me.

Mommy gaped at her helpless child on the floor, a girl coiled in a circle of angst and emotional disarray. The memories remain still.

"Learned your lesson?" she asked callously.

This was not about sorry Teddy is gone. This was not about remorse. This was emotional brutality. I was woozy with loss. I don't remember her exact words. She spoke simplistically, in a way I, a shaky girl, would understand.

She never touched me or tried to comfort me in any way.

Her words beat at me like the rat-a-tat sound of a machine gun.

"Never love, or you'll get hurt," she cautioned, her beautiful face scrunched in revolt. I never answered Mommy then. I knew that our gloomy house was an ongoing battleground and that life at home was war.

I was frozen in fear. She had loved and had her heart broken. She would teach me what a broken heart felt like. I'd loved Teddy much too much. She had to break my heart before a man did.

"Never answer back," was her next warning.

Much later, I thought I'd be a marionette, a girl with no backbone, no thoughts, no will. Having no backbone meant I could be used, taken for granted, disrespected. I'd be a puppet. I didn't know that this issue would be a lifelong struggle heaped on me the day Teddy was taken.

I was defenseless, totally defeated.

Now, in retrospect, I think that Mommy was talking to Mommy about Mommy.

Then I started to cry again, whimper. I was a defenseless girl, too inconsolable to understand, much less care about or listen to her lovelorn philosophies.

Yet, because I loved her, I wanted to beg Mommy's forgiveness for being like the husband she hated so much.

I wanted to tell her I wasn't anything like Daddy.

I'm sorry that I played deaf. I wanted to say that.

I said nothing. I had no strength.

Instead, I stood up. I was shaky. My knobby knees, the ones that had supported my passionate race to rescue Teddy, did not support me. I had fallen on the sidewalk several times during that pursuit. My knees were cut, scraped, and scratched with dried blood. They gave way.

Mommy didn't care that I started to crumble.

"You're just like your father," she repeated with a weird smile.

I fell into a deep faint. It was a merciful blackout.

Chapter Three
Warning

I squatted on the worn linoleum in the sparse kitchen, in a corner, hidden in full view, my nose stuck in one of Daddy's discarded paperbacks. It was an intriguing concise dictionary, battered, a flurry of creased and worn gossamer pages thick with charismatic words.

Consulting a dictionary is a noiseless pursuit. I hadn't broken Daddy's don't-ever-speak edict. I was temporarily safe, sound, and silent

When I clutched that old dictionary, a delightful dose of lightning zipped through me with a tenderness usually not associated with the real thing. I felt a little buzz of joy. I forgot I was a dumbbell. The ghost of Teddy was on the floor, snuggled against me.

I was busy looking up one word in the dictionary, soul. What was soul? Where does soul exist? I fingered the page anxiously until the answer peered back: "Soul is the spiritual or immaterial part of a human being or animal, regarded as immortal."

This sounded otherworldly.

I read it again. I memorized it.

I loved anything that smacked of the supernatural. I was a needy girl. I needed more of everything because I had nothing. Now the dictionary said I, a dumbbell, had a soul. How does a soul function? And what does the word "immortal" mean? I was trying to put together the pieces of this spiritual mystery. I needed instructions on how to access my soul, find out where it existed.

Clatter, I heard a strange clatter. It came from Mommy's direction. I looked up. She'd been sipping tea, and when she put the cup back in the saucer, it rattled louder than a nervous rattlesnake.

Mommy was shaking.

She was a natural psychic riddled with weirdly accurate premonitions. She was especially acute to Daddy's oncoming presence. When he was somewhere close but unseen, when he had descended into a dangerous kind of slyness that preluded a mean scheme, she sensed it.

Mommy's eyes were wide with fear. She started waving her wrists outwardly, frantically, in a get-out, get-lost gesture. Mommy was admonishing me to move, to hide, to disappear, to get out of his way.

I was glued to the floor, to the dictionary, to the moment. I was depleted. I'd just scrubbed down the whole kitchen. My hands hurt. My existence hurt. My heart hurt. Danger loomed, but I was too tired to take Mommy seriously. I was in denial.

She knew that seconds were ticking away. I hadn't changed my position. I was reckless. I continued to fidget among the pages of the dictionary, stubborn in my idiotic belief that an intermission instigated by me could delay a Daddy disaster.

Mommy's last resort was to spew a familiar tornado of words she knew that always burned me. "When you're happy, it's always a sign you're going to be sad." I used to think she was quoting a Chinese fortune cookie.

Now I knew better. We were stuck on the edge of a Daddy fit.

Mommy's next words sounded spilled out like a deranged drama.

"Happiness crushes little girls like you," Mommy ranted in fast speak. "Happiness is like an octopus. It has eight slithery arms that are like long poisonous snakes that seize you and mangle you."' She stopped to catch her breath. "They strike you with a toxin that looks like black ink. They squeeze the guts out of your body."

Mommy spewed these dark-dark scare tactics as if they were god's honest truth.

Mommy issued a final alert poetically, three little words that shook me to my senses.

"Foe is woe," she warned.

Oh, I knew woe.

Oh, I knew foe.

Daddy was my fiercest foe.

Daddy wasn't an octopus or a snake.

Oh my god! There he was, a mammoth elephant rumbling into the room.

Suddenly and stealthily, without preamble, Daddy zoomed into the kitchen from out of nowhere, the epitome of manly strength and speed, using the element of surprise as a tool mightier than a grenade.

Daddy was the alpha male, a Hercules who collected guns. He ruled by fear. I was his linchpin.

The issue?

I'd overheard him telling Mommy, constantly and vehemently, that I wasn't "submissive" enough. Daddy was a dictator. He was always bent on incapacitating me, making me a far lesser person than I was meant to be.

To underline the edict that this house was his dominion and that I was under his jurisdiction, he put Mommy and me under constant surveillance. Daddy liked to catch his two victims unaware, punish them first with an initial dread of some unknown upcoming vengeance. Then came the vengeance itself.

A chilling thought shivered through my subconscious. He was here to make a correction. I was going to be penalized. He looked at Mommy. Her lips were clamped shut. I was a rigid block of ice hot with fear.

"She is a dumbbell!" he shot the words at Mommy with a killer's precision, as if my idleness and, worse, a girl who'd recycled his discarded dictionary, was all her fault.

Daddy was tall and muscled, a formidable brawny giant. He fastened his gaze on me, a female thief who'd stolen a book, his book. He'd caught me red-handed, defenseless.

The tidbit of happiness I'd felt before this confrontation turned into an imperceptible smoke, putrid, that burned my eyes. Daddy eyed the dictionary scornfully. He oozed rancor. He looked like a rancher about to make his hot iron mark on a thin-skinned girl.

Then, came the vengeance.

Vengeance burns.

Chapter Four
Splitting

It got very, very still, as if the kitchen were an empty theater.

Daddy celebrated his wickedness, reveled in it. He liked surprise maneuvers. I was defenseless. I thought he was going to hit me. I flinched without moving.

He'd been loitering over me, a towering hulk when, swiftly, he reached down, grabbed the substantial dictionary from my hands, and, in one fell swoop, shred it in half as easily as if it were a piece of tissue paper.

"A dumbbell is all you'll ever be," he boomed malevolently, glaring at me, unmoving, each hand holding each half of the dictionary. He thrust the halves in my face and didn't move.

The grim message was clear. Daddy had demonstrated, without words, that what he did to that dictionary he could do to Mommy and me: tear us in half. Terror grabbed at me and didn't let go.

What made him go nuts was that I, a girl scrunched on the floor, was hooked on a book. Girls and books, especially a dictionary, do not belong together. Our house, *his* house, was a battle zone, and he'd found me hunkered down, on *his* territory, in his kitchen, on his floor, with *his* paperback dictionary.

My bad book behavior, combined with what he assumed was laziness, was high on his long list of no-nos. He never considered that I was simply exhausted, a slave in solace, before he went on the attack.

In my heart, I knew two things to be true.

When Daddy called me a dumbbell or, worse, when he referred to me vaguely, as "She," it meant that I was non-existent. But I was not a dumbbell. I had a real name. I also knew that icepick words like dumbbell are knives, swords, and daggers meant to maim and kill the spirit. The biggest lie I've ever heard goes back to 1862 when someone silly wrote in a periodical. "Sticks and stones will break my bones, but words will never hurt me."

Daddy's loathing of me, his blazing words, daggered my heart, slashed my soul, and pummeled my waning spirit.

When I was emotionally wounded, I fantasized. I fell into a brief spell of my own making. I pretended that another dumbbell, not me, hung her head. I stepped outside myself. All this was her fault. The evidence of her crime, a dictionary, was found in her hands, not mine.

The girl, the other girl, knew that reading books was bad. She'd be burned for her badness. She was a criminal caught red-handed. Home was already a jail. But there were other jails. Smaller jails. Locked cells. That's probably where she was headed. She was, after all, a book thief.

This eerie imagining happened faster than a blink and ended just as quickly. I was back in the war zone, the kitchen, compressed to the worn linoleum I'd just scrubbed.

Daddy pointed his forefinger at me, the real me, held it there, and his hostility was palpable. He turned his head toward Mommy and spoke like an oppressor speaks, with a tongue that slashes. "This is all your fault," he sneered. "The dumbbell is here to clean the house," He paused to watch Mommy wilt. "And you gave her time off to consult a dictionary? Is that how I told you to bring her up?"

Mommy's reply was no reply.

Daddy raised his voice several octaves.

"Are you allowing her to become literate?" he roared the contemptible words at Mommy with a killer's precision.

Oh yes, I yearned for literacy. Oh yes, I wanted to be among the literati.

I was a stupid fool when I should have been a sneak. If only I'd hidden the dictionary under my bed, stretched out in the dark, and read it with a stolen flashlight. I'd been too transparent.

Daddy fastened his gaze back on me again. I was petrified. Abruptly, I vanished into Daddy's imperceptible smoke, foul. It burned my eyes. The scorched tears didn't spill. Who'd care anyway? This was happening at home. What happens at home stays at home, behind closed doors.

I went inward again. It was harder this time. I got queasy. Vomit gurgled toward my throat. Daddy sensed the stifled terror of his girl captive. He built on it. That's what cowards do. That's what assassins do.

He returned his rabid attention to poor Mommy and lowered his voice as if I wasn't within earshot.

"She is a dumbbell with a *dictionary*?" he grunted as if he was a deity judging a far-reaching mortal sin by his firstborn, a daughter he preferred had been born a son. "This breaks my rules," he accused Mommy. "Books and girls were not made for each other. I told you that."

I could hear the spasmodic huffs and puffs of his escalating anger, the kind that leads to massive heart attacks. His fists were clenched. Deep wrinkles of contempt dug across his brow.

I hated Daddy. I hated home bullying and the emotional abuse that was exploding in this awful house. I hated that I, a targeted victim, was paralyzed.

Hate consumed me when he said my badness was all Mommy's fault. I loved Mommy. I didn't want to hurt her. My sins, oh I was so bad, were not her fault.

Mommy knew his coldblooded fit wasn't over. She stood rigidly in place, face immobile, like a trained soldier guarding Buckingham Palace. She was waiting for Daddy's next verbal attack.

"Is this what I told you to do with the dummy?" Daddy badgered her viciously in a damning tone.

Daddy's "dummy" abbreviation burned my burn. It was meant to convey to me, and to her, that I was in a class infinitely lower than a dumbbell.

I was going out of my mind, buckling, falling apart. I wanted to run away. You can never run faster than a tsunami. Panic flickered in my eyes and dissolved. Mommy knew that when I was cornered I could collapse into some loony inner tangent in a split second.

That's what I did whenever there was no escape from reality. That's what I did now. I fiddled inside myself, hunted down a speck of fortitude or, at least, resilience and hid in that safe haven.

Brandished by fear, my imagination soared. I saw myself at an easel painting a Daddy portrait. His face was a hideous Halloween monster mask that didn't peel off. Tightly suppressed laughter exploded within me. It was unexpressed hysteria, lunacy in its infancy.

My psychosis, if that's what it was, scrambled my mind, which raced hither and thither. Then, abruptly, my thoughts changed course. I was gripped, then gnawed, by an absurd sense of repentance.

Say sorry—sorry—sorry. Say it! Say it! Say it!

I was talking to myself without talking.

The sorry equation disappeared in a microsecond.

I was not remorseful. I was guilty of nothing. Daddy bound me in spiritual shackles. My only defense, the only way to soften the upsurge of his high-risk anger was that I, his target, apologize. It would be a pretend apology, false, but it might end Daddy's charade.

The word "sorry" prattled in my brain. So did resentment.

I was turning into a fake. The apology came out fake.

I blathered "sorry," and the word sputtered out unintelligibly sounding like baby babble. My tongue became rigid.

Daddy, whose ultimatum was always docility, heard no apology. I had refused to yield to him. I stood up to Daddy while sitting down. I was way too young to figure out that not apologizing properly while under dangerous Daddy duress was a sign that within my soul I harbored a burgeoning streak of bravery.

This was my first notion of what having a soul meant. A soul seemed to be an invisible bridge between what was real and what was imagined. The soul is where I could secret my secrets.

My girlish show of female independence, the first he'd seen, stoked his fire higher. Daddy didn't like my "sorry." It was a failure. I wasn't sufficiently meek. He disliked even more that I, the dumbbell, *his* dumbbell, was showing signs of becoming a defiant rule breaker. He was going to manipulate me into a soft target.

My wild imaginings took hold again.

I envisioned Daddy, the ultimate bully, standing over me, grunting like a grizzly bear standing on his hind legs ready to pounce. A supreme controller always sees, and seizes on his victim's vulnerability. But he was canny enough, sophisticated enough, to know that he didn't have to hit me, paw me, or bite chunks out of me to burn me.

He ambushed Mommy with more burn words, more singes, directed at me.

"The dumbbell is pigheaded," he growled. "Her perversity has to be destroyed." His voice was stern, even evil. "She's got to be tamed."

Daddy plunged each half of the ripped dictionary parts, one in each jacket pocket, now bulging, and stomped out of the kitchen.

The door blasted shut.

The house quivered under his enormous force.

Chapter Four
Second Thoughts

When the house turned deadly quiet again, a frantic thought hit me.

Maybe Mommy's recent show of reluctance to defend me was a significant cautionary, that she was already in the tame business.

Mommy expressed a perverse pleasure at my feverish breakdown when my doggie was kidnapped. That was taming. She never tried to interfere or stop Daddy's irrational rule of silence. That was taming. Just now, she did nothing to interfere with his dictionary damning but, then, we were both in danger and both afraid we'd be beaten.

My intuition, or whatever this snap judgment was, could be the seed of bigger obstructions meant to stop me in my tracks, anchor me when I didn't want to be anchored.

Mommy had become weaker and weaker. She could be coerced into becoming Daddy's cohort, his co-tamer. If this happened, it would be like two conquistadors joining forces.

I'd be a victim of torture in tandem.

Earlier that day, she had burned me externally, with iodine. It stung badly, like a bunch of bees blitzing me simultaneously. Maybe today's external Mommy burn was a sign that she was capable of more consequential burning, like burning away any chance for me to be me.

I was lost. I needed a savior. I needed direction born of wisdom. I needed to know how to mine the best of me. I had to exit the dumbbell world.

I had hidden my swollen hands under the now destroyed dictionary. My bony fingers were now in full view. They were puffy, scratched willy-nilly from scrubbing the oven with prickly steel wool. Whenever Mommy saw the slightest incision, she'd sprint to the medicine cabinet, a battered metal box with a cracked mirrored front. It was ugly. I was ugly. Ugly had consequences.

Iodine was Mommy's favorite antiseptic.

It sat in a half-used bottle on the first shelf, to the right, beside the preventive nail-bitter medicine prescribed by the ear doctor. Iodine burned. The nail potion brushed on my nail beds, ignited my lips, blistered them, and scalded my tongue. I burned when I bit my nails.

These were the first two medicinal monsters known to me. Mommy had used both on me that day. I tried not to react to the anguish of exterior burns. To stiffen my courage, I pretended what burned me didn't burn at all.

I didn't know that I was practicing the rudiments of stoicism. I didn't know that fortitude, in varying degrees, would ultimately be a part of my character even when I was at my weakest.

But in that dark moment, with nothing left, still sitting on the floor, I thought: I have guts. Some day I'll kill myself. That takes the most guts of all.

In the span of a moment, bursting into the labyrinth of both ears, I heard a far-away note of music. It came from a lyre, an ancient Greek harp that seemed to strum and stretch one-word on one string: "Nooooooo!"

The "no" signal didn't register. I had no idea where it came from or what it meant.

I had stayed on the floor just as I was, this time without my precious book, *his* book, trying not to think suicide. Oh! I shuddered in silence. If I could take the book back, snatch it, somehow rescue it, I would mend it, keep it, read it, treasure it.

Mere minutes passed. A quick premonition dropped down from nowhere and landed in my subconscious. Daddy's exit was a ploy. He was still around somewhere.

Beware! Beware!

Chapter Five
Bigger is Better

Daddy was a man of studied deception, a rogue who thrived on subterfuge as a tool to create an atmosphere of severe intimidation. He thrived on flaunting his absolute sovereignty. He loved to exude great physical power over the two helpless females in his house.

I'd inherited Mommy's sense of precognition, it was only a feeling, but I knew, somehow, that Daddy was still around, still close, still within earshot.

I braced myself.

It turned out that he had closed the door from the inside, making us assume that he'd left. He remained in the house, hiding, lurking in wait to hear what Mommy said or did, or what I said or did.

Daddy was ready to lunge back at us, at *me*.

Moments later, when he sprinted back into the kitchen, he found us in the exact position in which he'd found us the first time around, minus the dictionary.

I gaped. Mommy shivered. I looked in the direction of the newly-scrubbed sink wondering if, some happy day, I could drown myself in it if I plugged the stopper filled it with water, put my head inside, then didn't move no matter what. I looked at Daddy, my crazy Daddy, who was making me crazy.

He had our huge city phone book in his hands, a massive yellow thing, as broad and as thick as an encyclopedia. He was so satisfied with himself, how he'd taken us aback again, that he became smug. He smiled briefly, fiendishly.

Then he flexed his massive muscles, held the fat-fat telephone directory over his head, high, and tore it in half as effortlessly as he'd torn the dictionary. This time he kept the two halves held high, each half grasped in each hand. One half of the telephone represented me. The other half represented Mommy.

We were being shown, once again, in a more substantial way, how we could both be rent asunder. This was Daddy's idea of symbolism or visualization, maybe both, that he could cause our demise easily by breaking each of us in half.

The kitchen was no longer a kitchen. It was the facsimile of a wrestling ring.

Daddy's message was painfully clear. Watch out. Life is easily snuffed out.

He could break us in half, or choke us, twist our necks, or suffocate us, kill us just like he'd just murdered the dense phone book. His show of strength, bold and brash, spoke louder than words.

After he destroyed *his* dictionary and then the thick telephone book, I thought that he could punch the house, the whole house, with just one big shattering whack and it would collapse on us, annihilate us.

Daddy was tearing us apart. We were becoming more and more unstable. Our physical demise at his hands was, to him, as inconsequential as destroying the big overweight phone book, effortless and speedy.

The second slammed door was for real.

He was really gone, vanished.

Mommy made me check.

I looked out the front window. Daddy was strutting down the street, greeting neighbors benignly like the benevolent god they thought he was. They responded with deference. He was a big donor to all their religious and political causes.

First, he grabbed the two dictionary halves out of his jacket pockets and dumped them into an almost-empty sidewalk rubbish barrel as tall as me.

Plop. Plop.

Then he dropped in the telephone halves.

Bang, bang.

The man was a fanatic bigot, a classic chauvinist. We, his two women, were always subject to his will, his fits and his kingship.

The emotional terrors he engendered within the house were not disposable. They stayed within the house, lurked within its gloomy walls. The fear he engendered followed me everywhere. As I tell you all this, I can still feel pangs of panic belting me.

Later, when civility returned, Daddy always justified his rages by assuring Mommy that little girls like me have to be curtailed when they're young.

"The dumbbell will be putty in my hands one day," he gloated.

I didn't know much about putty.

I wondered if putty burned.

Chapter Seven
Reminisces

Daddy never asked where I found *his* book, the first one he trashed.

I'd discovered the dictionary by accident.

I was cleaning *his* den. When I emptied *his* wastebasket, I saw the discarded dictionary strewn among a maze of stinky remnants from *his* ashtray, smelly stubs of stomped-out, Stogies from Cuba. Daddy liked world-class luxury goods if they were for him.

The dictionary I pulled out of the trash smelled stale. I didn't care. I placed it over my heart. It was something precious, a book that defined words I wanted to use in a way that was still one of my unknowns.

Just before Daddy tore the dictionary in half, I'd been concentrating hard on that four-letter word, soul. I wanted to know where, in the human body, the soul existed. It was not an organ, like a liver or lungs. The dictionary gave examples of how the word, soul, was used in common phrases like "body and soul" and "heart and soul."

Immediately before Daddy's kitchen chaos, I was thinking that I had two hearts.

One heart pumps the blood that keeps me alive.

The second heart, invisible as a vapor, was my soul. It was tucked unseen somewhere inside me. It housed my spirit, my intuition, and my instincts. The definition included the word immortal.

I didn't know what immortal meant. But the dictionary was gone. I mourned for it as if it was alive and had died.

It was within this wanton imaging that an illogical inkling whammed itself into my thoughts. It came from nowhere and held me in its thrall. It heightened my eyesight. I could see what wasn't there, what was everywhere.

One thousand angels, 1,000 of them, were drifting around me. They floated down effortlessly to my low level from somewhere in the upper strata of the universe, that huge desert upstairs, the sky. They, whatever "they" were, had alighted in my space to protect me, to communicate with me, and to mentor me. I don't know how I identified them as angels. They weren't stereotype angels.

The imagery, totally preposterous, was make-believe.

In hindsight, I think that my 1,000 angels, an army of them who occupied one of the vast unknowns, heard me crying out, reaching out, wanting out by some sort of suicide. Maybe they knew my Daddy disconnect. Maybe they were assigned to me by some invisible Power who knew the creative me, my love for fantasies, the unreal.

I was a dreamer, a believer in fables, a girl who let the word "suicide" dance on her brain, when what she really wanted was to live and work in a world where books and paintings ruled.

It was in this humble house shrouded with dark green shingles, the one that stood kitty-corner in a crowded city neighborhood studded with old three-deckers, that I was growing up.

Some houses, the colors of bitter chocolate or a waning

dark green Christmas tree, had peeling paint. Some houses also had distorted chain link fences with crawl spaces. They were crumbling three-deckers that seemed to lean into each other. So did the windows. My nosy neighborhood was an open stage.

I was maturing in a world without grass, without flowers, without friends, without talking, without heart, and without Mommy, the way she used to be when I was a little girl.

Chapter Eight
Self-Worth

Daddy convinced Mommy that housework was far more important than homework. Whenever he caught sight of my schoolbooks, he fumed. One evening, while drinking some concoction Daddy gleaned from his small bar, I heard him tell her: "Teach the dumbbell a real lesson."

He knew I'd hear the threat through closed doors.

I'd done nothing to arouse Daddy's ire. I didn't know why his awful outrage centered on me, what caused it to erupt with a punishment I did not deserve. I always cleaned good, real good, because I was afraid of a Daddy boomerang or, as it turned out, a "taming."

The next day, I rushed in from school, books in hands, ready to run upstairs to my little room to study.

Mommy was blocking the staircase.

She thrust under my nose a smelly used potty from a highchair baby, a girl. The child belonged to one of Daddy's political pals, a man who promised his wife their year-old baby would have a nice home while they were on a

Caribbean cruise.

I knew nothing of this plan or that I was to be a caretaker.

Daddy's politico would owe him a big favor. When Mommy eventually asked Daddy to share the fee, he told her it would be paid "another way." I overheard everything. The house was small, the walls thin, and Daddy was loud.

The potty stank. Loose stools floated in old urine. I didn't look at it again. I held my breath. "This is what you are," Mommy added, wild-eyed, looking up from the excrement to my stunned face. I rushed to the upstairs toilet to flush away the mess. Hurt feelings aren't so easily disposed.

When I came downstairs, the dirty potty was washed clean. Mommy, always fighting her conscience, always fighting nervous breakdowns, ordered me to start ironing a pile of baby clothes stashed in a frayed wicker hamper she kept in the cellar.

"It's your duty," she harrumphed, repeating a familiar phrase Daddy used on her often, too often, and it had driven her mad. When she resisted one of Daddy's orders, he always said the same thing. "It's your duty." Now the rule of duty was passed down to me.

I was ironing a ruffled baby dress when the loose handle of the old iron twisted on its base and, searing red hot, landed on my inner left wrist. It scorched away a large patch of skin.

I jumped back suddenly, racked with pain. When I started to wail, I was shushed. "You'll wake the baby," Mommy scoffed. I was in excruciating pain. That's when I discovered that burn by words and burn by fire are different burns that produce the exact same effect: torture.

Mommy didn't move from her perch, an armchair where she sat crocheting calmly. She told me to get some Vaseline from the medicine cabinet. The Vaseline made the burn worse. I bandaged it myself. In lieu of actual bandages, Mommy always left a bunch of small clean rags torn from a discarded sheet in a shoebox nearby.

I hurt. The burn hurt. My head hurt. My heart hurt. My world hurt.

The next day my homeroom teacher noticed the anguish on my face and the primitive rag knotted across my left wrist. She sent me to the school nurse. The burn had become a reddish-brown char. I winced when she removed the rag that stuck piteously to the sticky ointment.

When I began to gag, the nurse rushed me to a small sink and held my forehead until the vomiting was over. She spread a soothing salve on my burn, bandaged it properly, and gave me an aspirin.

"Thank you," is all I could manage. "Thank you."

"How did you get burned?" the nurse prodded. She didn't know that a vow of silence had been forced on me. When I didn't answer, she became suspicious. She sensed my sorrow and became thoughtful and quiet, like me.

Every day that nice school nurse checked my burn, re-bandaged it, and assured me everything was going to be all right. I was a dumbbell. I was born bad. I thought bad things happened only to me. I wished I could tell the nurse my true feelings about being the focus of emotional abuse. Daddy would kill me if I spoke out, break me in half like he did to the dictionary and the telephone book.

But, for a moment standing there, in the nurse's office, I longed that Mommy would treat me like the nurse treated me, with kindness. I wished Mommy cared about me again. I wished she cared when I was sick. I wished and wished and while the wishing was in full swing, the nurse patted me on the shoulder and walked me back to class.

I knew Mommy, poor Mommy, couldn't or wouldn't revert to her true self. Once upon a time, she treated me as if I were precious to her. I still didn't know why Mommy had changed so much, why the sight of me brought her such obvious unhappiness.

That seemed like a long, long time ago, before Mommy got involved with gypsies.

Chapter Nine
Forecasts

Mommy's irrationalities were linked to her devotion to mysticism.

She was superstitious to a fault.

Once, for no reason, she gave me a family heirloom, a pinkie ring embedded with a small heart-shaped diamond attached to a sapphire about the same size and style. "You are the diamond, I am the blue part," she said in a rare kindness. We locked glances. Glints of gratitude shone in my eyes. She was telling me, in her way, that I still had a chance to shine. This was my good luck charm. It still is.

I was not allowed to speak, to express my gratitude, so I just kept my eyes trained on Mommy. "You can always make sense out of nonsense," she added sweetly. For a split second, the undiluted mother-daughter love of my childhood came to life.

Then she walked away.

I understood her marital plight. I lived it. I was

punished for being an integral part of it. I didn't know the "how" or "why" of my feeling that I was born a discard. In Daddy's absence, I tried to ask questions. They were ignored. Instead, Mommy handed me a used Ouija Board, which I never touched. "Find out things for yourself," she quipped senselessly with a wry smile.

Mommy liked esoteric games that offered prognostications about life ahead. Her everyday favorites were Tarot cards, runes, and the messages someone read from coffee ground shapes left in emptied cups turned upside down. She did the same thing with tea leaves.

Gypsy predictions were something else.

She thought gypsies had some form of extra-terrestrial telepathy that emanated from unchartered sources and, therefore, rang true. Gypsy forecasts were more comforting to Mommy than happy pills or happy drinks.

Slowly but surely I was absorbing by osmosis, a deep-rooted belief in sympathetic magic, especially the idea of the existence of my 1,000 angels. I never let on that I had abstract entities around me or that we corresponded about issues Mommy never acknowledged.

Mommy had a neighbor-pal, Mary, who liked gypsy jaunts too. Her policeman husband was an alcoholic who, following a bender, beat her senseless with his wooden nightstick. Some blows were averted. Too many were not. When the tempest blew out of control, Mary gleaned rescue covertly, wherever and however she could.

Once, during a beating scenario, Mary ducked a blow and, in the process, got a glimpse of me sweeping the front porch stairs. She flew out of her patched-up screen door and put a scribbled scrap of white paper in my hand. "Give it to your mother," she pleaded before sprinting back through the same door, back to hell.

I noticed slap welts on her face. Her arms were badly bruised. She held one at a funny angle. It was badly swollen. Maybe it was broken. Oh, I thought, as I ran in the house to find Mommy, there are different kinds of burns. Some burns destroy your innards. Some burns destroy your outers.

Mommy refolded the paper, which I never looked at, put it tightly in my fist, and told me to run fast-fast to a nearby Catholic rectory.

"Get a priest," she said. "Speed it up. Give him the paper."

It was a time when police didn't respond enthusiastically to brother policemen committing assault and battery at home. No. They bristled at being hauled into court to defend their buddies, the wife beaters.

Besides, there was no 911.

There was only me, the dumbbell, on an emergency rescue to locate a priest, any available priest, to break up this marital rage and, later, neutralize it with a contrite confession.

By the time I ran back home, the priest had already pulled up in a sleek black Ford and was rushing through the same saggy screen door that shielded a husband beating his wife. Diplomacy and negotiation with a madman takes time. It was bedtime when I looked out of my one small window and saw the priest pull his car away—but not before he threw the policeman's spooky nightstick into his trunk.

Mary and Mommy loved to hunt down itinerant gypsy fortunetellers who existed in temporary tents in the woods off major highways. When it was broad daylight and emotionally dark at home, they both begged for assurances that the upcoming forecast centered on the sunny side of life.

The two women, one plain and one gorgeous, talked between themselves about husbands abusing wives, the how of it, and the why of it. Daddy never hit Mommy. But I think Mary heaped a gruesome fear on top of Mommy's spiraling trepidation about Daddy's tantrums. She made Mommy feel that Daddy was capable of assault and battery.

When we went gypsy hunting, Mommy parked behind bushes, on grassy slopes. She thought someone might see the car, squeal its identity and location to Daddy. She muzzled me when I climbed out of the back seat, put her hand over my mouth, and raised her eyebrows. She brought shushing to a new level.

I didn't care.

My eyes and ears absorbed everything easily. When I trailed Mommy and her friend to gypsy land, it was with far more curiosity and emotional freedom than they assumed a bullied girl harbored.

The soothsayers, the gypsies, were bohemian women who scarfed their heads, ringed their eyes black, wore circular maxi dresses sewn together from rags that no quilter would touch. They had dirty bare feet, smelled bad, and predicted futures by fingering the palm.

Mommy and Mary both thought the gypsies had some mystical link to ancient prophets. Mommy listened to predictions in rapt attention. There had to be something more to life than Daddy. Mary listened with distrust. She'd been beaten too many times. But a gypsy always offered tantalizing tidbits twined in hope. That's what these two distraught women craved: hope.

The gypsies seemed like costumed actors, waiting for a curtain to open, waiting for their benefactor's money. Their posturing of self-importance was fascinating. They acted as if they knew about major things, future things, good things

What raced through my mind was that Mommy was spending tight household money to hear useless forecasts about a Daddy acting badly. They predicted he was going to change.

The gypsies were ignorant impostors.

Daddy never changed.

Chapter Ten
Silence

What hurled me down and kept me stuck on that black brick road, was Daddy's abolitionist command. "Remain silent under all circumstances," he'd snarled. "No exceptions."

Speechlessness was a cruel confinement. I felt as if a ruthless knife-wielder had hacked my vocal cords and stolen my tongue. It was so real that I had a perpetual sore throat. Now and then, my lips opened as words formed and suddenly slipped back to wherever words begin. I fiddled with the idea of "cheat talk" when Daddy wasn't around. I knew if Mommy heard a slight muttering, she'd tattle.

She'd become fragile and more and more susceptible to Daddy's weird coercions.

When I weighed the impact of Daddy's nutty rules, my indigo state of mind got even darker. One day, Daddy followed me to the kitchen, plunked me down on a wooden chair, and laid down his irrefutable rules again. He began by telling me he was doing this because dumbbells don't get things right the first time.

"Never answer back," he recapitulated.

I never did. Mommy had already laid down that rule.

People judged me to be stupid or shy, or both. Pretty soon, they ignored me. My sense of isolation had rocketed until I became a close-mouthed shell of my real self.

"Never ask or answer a question." Daddy continued.

I never did, except when I talked to myself without making a sound.

I'd heard my teacher confide to one of her colleagues that I never raised my hand, or participated in class activities, but got good grades anyway. "How does she do it?" my teacher wondered.

"Never express an opinion."

I never did.

Daddy, who liked my flourishing passivity, confided to Mommy: "See, I told you she was putty." Mommy nodded once and stared at the floor. She didn't express opinions either.

"Never issue a request."

I never did.

I knew of no one who'd honor my most trivial plea. I never asked for anything from anybody. Being incommunicado gave me a feeling of incarceration. My wounds, oh they ran deep, were bottled up inside me. I had no outlet, no guidance. I was an angry ball of bitter indignation, a disenfranchised girl on the verge of becoming a disenfranchised teen.

There was a light flickering at the end of the tunnel.

I was blind to it.

Yet thoughts about silence, my brutish silence, assaulted me.

I thought, *silence is the ultimate silencer.* I thought, *silence blocks the story it hides, forces the truth of the unknown into the grime of oblivion.* I thought, *someday I'll decode my silence. I'll give my silence a luminous voice.*

I laughed. It wasn't comedic laughter. It was a silent

wail of frenzy.

I was still too young, too withdrawn, to consider that being forbidden to talk would ultimately heighten all my senses. What I heard and saw took on the patina of transparency. I could see through people and situations. I heard what was left unsaid. I could hear what people were thinking.

Daddy's forced withdrawal from everyday communication gave me the gift of lucidity, of being able to write fastidiously about what I was prohibited to speak. It didn't occur to me that I was being strengthened to rely on inner strengths, hone them, so that I could maneuver or bypass or crash through life's obstacles.

But then my feelings were murky. I thought I had a full-blown virus that had no antibiotic cure. I cowered. My insides churned. Confusion rattled my core. My resentment was raw. I was like a distraught prisoner who couldn't locate an escape hatch.

I ruled out face-to-face rebellion. I could easily be torn in half, like the telephone book. That reality made me more bereft, unstable. Sometimes, when I talked to myself, I said: "Hey, you're like a dead girl walking."

Daddy not only controlled my comings and goings, he became my monarch. He wanted a puny, helpless girl viable to strings that he controlled. I was his pawn, his dupe.

He was the man who reduced me to nobody.

I'd slipped through the cracks while impounded in an accessible place: home. I wasn't worth saving. I was an expendable dumbbell. I couldn't scream for help. Who'd care anyway?

I was set apart, cast aside, hidden, and banished. I was burned out. I wanted out. Suicide! Suicide! Suicide! I wanted to be a suicide. I sketched a plan. I could drink either from Mommy's iodine bottle or swallow fingernail fluid. Both beckoned. Both had already burned me outwardly. Maybe I could die of internal burns.

Burn was what a dumbbell deserved. Burn! Burn!

Burn!

When I inched nearer and nearer to committing suicide, some strange whimsy, some unidentifiable intermediary, made me face my own truth.

I didn't have the guts to burn my guts. I was a wimp, a "fraidy cat."

What I really wanted was to die softly, softly without murdering myself or being murdered.

I was made of putty.

Daddy was right.

Chapter Eleven
Two Victims

Mommy began mumbling under her breath more frequently than ever.

What she said was usually garbled. She murmured the same unintelligible gibberish over and over, in vague singsong.

Finally, she spoke out, to me, to the heavens, to anyone within hearing distance, anyone who cared about her plight. "He is a street angel and house devil," she screamed and burst into inconsolable tears.

It was true. She'd said that a million times before. She'd wept before. But not like this. She wept like I'd wept for Teddy, with wanton abandon. I wanted to hug Mommy, tell her everything would be all right.

She didn't want my hugs anymore. She didn't want me. She kept me at arm's length, shied away from visible affection. She became Victorian in her ways, standoffish and infinitely more prudish than I would have believed. Her great beauty, with which she dazzled men, remained intact. All it took from her to melt a man was a casual glance or a half-smile.

Mommy was changing. She was a stifled and suppressed suffragette who didn't even know she was a suffragette. She was one of masses of downtrodden women who couldn't possibly envision that one fine day Feminism would take the world by storm.

The truth was that this era was neither Mommy's time nor my time.

The hate I felt toward Daddy consumed me. Mommy had limited influence if she didn't cross him. Me? I remained his Number One target. I was totally vulnerable to his whims. Daddy expected my unwavering deference. I was to be a prime example of how easily a man, a Daddy, can manipulate a woman, his young daughter.

I hated his unpredictable cruelty, how daunting he seemed.

I despised his extreme chauvinism, how it controlled his reason.

I detested his cutting manner of male supremacy. He thought females were born passive. They could be tread upon easily. If they progressed, he thought that they should be trampled before they got too far. When a woman was grounded, defeated, he rejoiced. Daddy was a king of chauvinism.

I loathed yielding to his assumed supremacy I was a frightened girl getting taller, getting leaner, getting prettier, getting smarter, gaining bits and pieces of wisdom here and there.

Inside, where spiritual strength really counted, I wasn't strong.

The emotional abuse heaped on me made me trust no one I was certain that everything I did, or tried to do, would end up in disappointment. I was a damaged girl, a misfit who held on, by a thread, to the belief that she wasn't a misfit.

I did not stand straight. I slouched in a toxicity of self-loathing. I didn't make eye contact with people. I was consumed by humiliation and a sense of worthlessness. When I walked, I looked at my shoes.

I didn't have a smidgeon of self-pride. When Daddy commanded me to shut up, I shut myself in because I felt shut out.

Once I overheard him tell Mommy that I was useable. "The day is coming when we can use the dumbbell," he'd bragged. I couldn't forget that he'd called me "putty."

I wanted to understand Daddy's "putty" implication more fully. There was a dictionary at the neighborhood library. When I was on a quick errand, like getting a 10-cents loaf of bread, I took a minute to dash into the library, look up the word and dash home without getting caught and, therefore, escaped retribution.

Putty is moldable, pliable.

The metaphor made my plight clearer. Daddy wanted a compliant daughter, a slave he could exploit. Daddy assumed that once putty, permanently putty. I was alone, boxed in, just what Daddy wanted, pliable.

Still, there was a fragment of self-respect bubbling inside me. I didn't want to become an emotionally distraught woman. When Mommy relinquished gypsies, she began sputtering, "I know my fate... I'm living my fate." Ah, that's why Mommy suddenly dropped the gypsies. One of them must have hit upon reality.

I told Mommy I would change my life someday and hers too. I hadn't heard my voice in a long time. I burbled, fast, afraid my absent Daddy might hear.

"Wishful thinking," Mommy responded. It was a dismissal. She'd surrendered to Daddy's laws. Her pessimism was real and profound. It was also infectious and insidious. It was like a germ that invaded, and stayed, to afflict those who live in close proximity.

I swore an oath to myself: I would not become another Mommy like mine, a woman beholden to, and totally dependent on a man like Daddy.

I did not know that my amazing grace wouldn't flower until I conquered me, all the things I could be.

One night, when I was washing a sink full of clattering dirty dishes, 1,000 angels showed up in the kitchen. I didn't see them. I heard them. They came together, joined themselves in one delightful choir, and sung in my ear. "You're not alone."

I was so needy, so beaten, I held tightly onto those words, not realizing that some words, although sweet, can be as slippery as a slab of ice.

Chapter Twelve
Intervention

I felt myself move. It was not of my own volition. I must be hallucinating. I was not in charge of myself. This strange spur-of-the-moment experience was way, way beyond my control.

A gentle jolt from nowhere took hold of me, and suddenly, with no warning, I was on a swing flying high, watching the earth vanish below. The swing just kept on moving up, up. I dangled through a puff of clouds. Swiftly, and as gently as the eagle flies heavenward, I was whisked to an unknown place, foreign, but I didn't feel like a foreigner.

I didn't know where it was located geographically. This strange escapade defied geography, globes, maps, clocks, and calendars. It was either a fantasy or a dream. There were no other humans, or any species, around. It was just I alone plunked on a high-up cliff somewhere, evaluating my fantasy landing as if the odd journey wasn't odd.

I heard mystifying musical sounds, wispy ones, floating toward me.

A flute? A harp? A violin?

I could sense, but not identify, the honeyed musical notes that danced in the atmosphere. It was as if the air embraced me without touching me. Then "they," some invisible sorcerers I did not know, communicated with me in my own language, words.

"Forget putty," I heard from a faraway choir that was tantalizingly close.

Pouty denials raced through my mind.

How can I forget putty? How can I forget that Daddy thinks of me as a dumbbell made of putty? How can I forget that Daddy has rendered me mute?

My rebuttal was the sullen musing of an emotionally crippled cynic, a helpless girl who didn't know where she was or what was happening.

The magical vibrations, or the chiming chorus or choir, or whatever or whoever these spell workers were, repeated their two-word communiqué more earnestly.

"Forget putty," sang the same chorale in a more commanding chord. Yet the melody was so gentle, so pleasing, so fluffy, and so brief that it brushed by my ears with a kiss as light as a ladybug landing.

What I heard, what I felt, was otherworldly. I was in another sphere. The sheer wonder of the moment ebbed and flowed as I sat stone still.

I was unused to beautiful places, beautiful things, and beautiful assurances. It was beyond comforting. I liked where I was, especially what I thought of as emotional pampering.

But old regrets, old criticisms, old berates, old orders of remaining mute and forgetting books don't perish easily. I was jinxed. Daddy's frequent aggressive brainwashing had a strong hold on me. I heard a moan. The moaning was coming from me without my making a sound.

I was in a good place, somewhere magnificent. But I

was suspicious of goodness. I thought happiness, even a temporary sliver of it, was a portent of sorrow, Mommy had drummed that thought into my head frequently.

My sense of inadequacy prevailed. I was riddled with doubts. Much better that I not put faith in a lovely place, lovely music, lovely assurances.

Besides, I didn't know what planet I was on. I didn't know anything about what, or who, my mind-reading liberators were. Burn! I could burn here.

Was this the forecasted kidnapping? Maybe!

Had I been drugged and whisked off by some baffling abstract entity?

Was I in the land of unknowns? Had I been thrust into a different civilization?

What was going on? Was I a hostage?

Yet, in spite of my doubts, love surrounded me. The love felt nicer than the skepticism. On a whim, I blocked my insecurities.

My champions listened to every nuance of every doubt, every dread, surging through my soul. Someone, or perhaps it was more than one someone, lifted the veil of ruination from my eyes. I gulped in awe.

I faced a vast outdoor room with a spectacular view.

Everything was peaceful and pretty, especially the rainbow of abundant exotic flowers that thrived on lime-colored bushes nestled next to archaic brown tree trunks gnarled with age. I felt a mellow wind caress me, soothe me. I smelled fresh gardenias. Only gardenias.

I couldn't believe I'd been transported to such an alluring wonderland.

Something in me, something stored in a place Daddy never reached, wanted to believe in beauty again, in integrity, in the potential of me. I wanted to trust that I'd find, or be helped to find, a way to turn a dumbbell into a dazzler.

I gazed at the beyond.

The flat ocean, a swath of silky-smooth turquoise, had a

horizon that fused into infinity. I was sitting on the high edge of a deep cliff, my feet dangling. If I let myself go, wiggled a little, I could commit suicide here and now. I didn't need to drink iodine or nail liquid to die.

But I held on, even though there was nothing real to hold onto, and only because I wanted to go on.

I was bluffing.

Suicide wishes shot me more times than I can count.

The angels, all 1,000 of them, delivered a simple message. Suicide would rob me of my chances. That's what the angels told me without telling me.

I began to consider that maybe there were chances in my future. The angels hummed that uncanny idea into my head. Life was all about creating chances, seizing chances, making the chances work on my behalf.

Was I having a change of heart? Was I thinking with my heart? Could a soul do that?

All I was aware of is that all the negatives that had been drummed into me were temporarily eased. I was told, or got the impression, that I had a place in the world, a fine place. I just had to unearth it.

That thought alone consumed me with a durable sense of peace I'd never experienced. It seemed to embrace me with an assurance still unknown to me. I begged to stay in this place of exquisite joy. I don't know whom I begged. I only know I begged imperceptible rescuers. The only answers I heard back were brief snippets of sweet woodwind music from the unknowns.

Maybe this was too much imagining.

Maybe I was a crazy girl.

I meandered between belief and disbelief. I went back and forth.

I got dizzy.

I thought: *this is an escape mechanism.* Bullied girls like me who come from homes where brash chauvinism reigns are often prone to unique illusions. Yet this moment was so dear, so personal, I wanted it to remain in my memory forever.

The vibrations, if that's what they were, shook me awake from my abstract distractions. Tranquility reigned. I thought I'd been drugged

In the near distance, I heard a clatter of gentle voices, jolly voices. They were just twitters, tweets, and from this delightful jibber-jabber, I got a message. I'd been craving suicide. This fantasy place, and whatever or whoever the forces around me were, represented a serious intervention.

I didn't really know how my mysterious mentors, those anonymous 1,000 angels, transported me to their territory. They had their own radar, their own fleet of flying saucers. They shined a glaring spotlight on me, and instead of being blinded by the intensity of 1,000 Klieg lights, I felt bathed in 1,000 watts of a strange sunshine that didn't burn.

Haunting questions consumed me. I said nothing.

The angels heard every syllable of every word bouncing on my brain.

How did the angels hear me utter the word "putty" when I didn't say it out loud?

How could they possibly know about Daddy's daunting condemnations, especially that horrible one about never speaking up? That happened between the four walls of the old house which needed more repair than me.

How were they able to descend, unseen, into that dreadful place where I lived? How could they possibly measure the scope and throb of my soul's pain? How did they know about the horrendous fear of kidnapping that had been thumped into my head from early childhood?

How did they highjack me so quickly, so soundlessly, so kindly?

"Forget kidnap," came the words issued on two brief flute notes.

I'd been referred to as dumbbell so many times, and with such condescension, that I began to think that these questions were whimsical figments of a dumbbell's ravished imagination

I have no idea where the idea came from, but I thought that everything has two sides. I'd just been given the golden gift of thinking about silver linings, about good things happening to a bad dumbbell.

The message came from fragments of music that had texts.

"Forget dumbbell," a flute sprinkled on the air

"Forget putty," came the wind-like advice of a violin.

"Forget being kidnapped," I heard from a mellow guitar.

"Forget threats," sang a harp.

"Forget words like no, like you cannot, like iodine, like burn," all the instruments played together, as if I were hearing chords of luscious Bach chamber music.

A thunderbolt thought hit me. It felt like the tickle of a feather.

"You will rise," is what I heard. Me? Rise?

I'd been hallucinating. That was it.

Now I was wide-awake.

Chapter Thirteen
The Glob

I narrowed my eyes into slits.

I willed them to mutate into an all-seeing camera lens.

I wanted an unobstructed view of the impossible midnight scene I was witnessing here, on earth, in my narrow bedroom, a wide-awake girl, snug under a quilt made of old rags treated as art by someone with a needle, thread, thimble, and patience.

Another fantasy was playing itself out at the foot of my banged-up antique bed.

What I saw, or what I thought I saw, was a wheel of shimmying white chiffon rectangles floating in a circle. Or was it a bunch of untoasted marshmallows strung together in the shape of a full moon going 'round and 'round?

No.

The circle came closer. I stared at it with as much intensity as I could martial. Was it a gaggle of white doves moving in ring formation?

No.

If these were my 1,000 angels, and I began to think they were, they were not facsimiles of angels found in cathedrals or museums. They weren't statue angels or cemetery angels. I saw no angel wings. No cherubs. No flowing robes. I saw no image that resembled angels on stain glass windows or angels painted on a Basilica ceiling by medieval masters of church art.

No.

The white circle rotating before me had great luminosity and an indescribable clarity. It didn't have eyes, but it saw right through me. It communicated with me voicelessly, and I heard everything, and, conversely, it heard me,

What was in my room, circling around my bed, were a glob of illuminators who held me in their thrall? I don't know who or what they were. I heard the word "faith" whispered as clearly as if it was shouted. I also got the idea that I was expected to rely on the supernatural, in what I didn't see, but knew existed.

Had I long, long ago tried to access these uncommon angels without knowing what I was looking for?

When I was sitting on the kitchen floor, hunting for the word "soul" in the dictionary Daddy destroyed, was I subconsciously reaching out for this entity, these 1,000 angels, as if they actually existed? I knew now they heard what was inaudible, what was going on in my mind. I, in turn, heard them speak to me from a glob that didn't have an ordinary voice. I could actually hear the unspeaking angels speaking to me.

Was it possible that the soul had its own acoustics?

Instantly I realized that my once-deaf ears could hear what was indistinct. My cubbyhole bedroom, the kitchen, any old place, became angel territory when the angels landed there.

"We're going to remove the heavy rock lumped on your splintered soul," is the way the angels summed up their presence.

Never had I known such transformative care. Never had such tenderness been heaped on me. I inhaled deeper than I'd ever inhaled. I inhaled *them*, the spirit of 1,000 angels comforting me.

The glob disappeared, just slipped through the glass windowpane without breaking it to smithereens. I jumped out of bed. I wanted to follow them. But they were gone, godly magicians riding across the sky in one white glob.

I saw them cavorting among the shooting stars, careening past the meteors, and shooing the man on the moon from his perch so they could rest there awhile.

They were so quiet as they did all these otherworldly things that I began to believe that the word silence, the word Daddy loaded on me, had a new perspective. I pondered the burgeoning miracle. My 1,000 angels in the glob had talked to me one more time in a basic, no-frills way.

"Silence, like sleep, heals and restores you," is what I heard.

Yes, I thought and, believing I'd somehow been hypnotized, slept soundly.

Chapter Fourteen
Piano

A deep sleep refused to relinquish its tight grip on me.

I was suspended somewhere mysterious, caressed by a vast swath of twilight, dreaming under that nice old warm quilt that had lots of mended holes.

My 1,000 angels never interrupted my dreams. They never shook me awake. They flitted around me soundlessly when I was asleep or not. I heard everything they said.

Someone was insisting that I sit up, get up, and get ready.

It was Mommy.

She shook my shoulders with too much enthusiasm. My head bounced. I awoke startled. I was woozy. Something important was happening. It was the middle of the night. Mommy still wore street clothes. She was smiling. Smiling! Mommy hardly ever smiled at me. Daddy was coming home with an unnamed guest, a friend of his, someone politically important who wanted me to play the piano and sing Irish lullabies.

I was in a daze. I dozed off again, sitting up, chin down.

What I heard didn't register.

Mommy shook me again. Instructions were issued. I heard the gist of Mommy's mumbles. I was to go downstairs, beam at Daddy's friend, sit at the second-hand piano, play, and sing Irish ditties. If Daddy's guest applauded, I was to continue my miniature repertoire.

I was a slow responder when roused from a deep sleep.

Mommy poked me in the ribs. "Do as you're told," she warned, using Daddy's harsh tone.

Suddenly I was wide-awake.

A bad feeling swept over me. Doom hovered in the shadows. A giant hand gripped my soul and squeezed hard. My heartbeat accelerated. Dread overtook me. I had a gloomy premonition. Something awful, something shocking, hung in the shadows of the night.

It was a scary foreboding. I can't explain its origin or how, or why, it nagged me.

Mommy was smiling again with honest-to-goodness delight. Her eagerness was not contagious. Something or someone, maybe it was my 1,000 angels, implied that Daddy was up to no good because Daddy was no good. He was a fraud, a charlatan, a tricky sham man. He could caress Mommy with his eyes and lie to her at the same time.

My 1,000 angels were clattering about me now, cautioning me, urging me to act cool, be smart, play the music but realize, and accept, that I was about to be rigged into something dishonest, something that appeared superficial but had enormous significance.

The hour was wrong.

The situation was wrong.

Mommy acted as if nothing was wrong. That in itself was wrong.

I don't know how, but my angels punched into my brain a stark defense: I had to be strong. I argued with them. Why did I have to be strong? I was just an inconsequential nothing.

Angels do not surrender to protests from an emotionally bungled girl.

"Truth!" I heard them whisper in unison.

And again: "You're going to hear the truth!"

The angels told me outright that I would have to face up to things, traumatic things, and if my heart were broken again, they would help me mend it. *Truth!* I was going to hear some god-awful truth and if I fainted under the weight of it, the angels would prop me up.

What I truly loved about my 1,000 angels is that they made me think that their guidance, the ideas they dropped on my path, really sprung from my perception, my wisdom. They jabbed me with a series of little jolts of courage that would slide me through a hard place.

I looked at Mommy again. She was still smiling. Even her eyes smiled. I had never seen her so excited about the way I played that old piano. Usually, Mommy ignored me completely, even when it mattered. I was the only child in my class who had no representative at parent-teacher meetings, *ever*.

My homeroom teacher eventually took me aside. "Why?" she asked.

I just stood there, a dismayed dumbbell engulfed in silence, gazing at the floor. I had begged Mommy to come to the school, and she turned as cold-hearted as Daddy. "I just don't care!" she'd jeered. I was so ashamed to stand so alone, so deserted, at these school meetings that I felt as disconnected in school as I did at home.

The teachers stopped asking questions. I saw them chatting among themselves and stop abruptly when I whisked by, headed toward the exit.

Now Mommy seemed to care. It had nothing to do with school.

I wanted to go back to bed. I didn't want to indulge Daddy. I had made promises to myself. They involved independence and escape. I'd been on an on-high cave, my hiding place. I knew I couldn't get there now. There was no escape from Daddy, or his conniving friend, who turned out to be a drunken old man.

It was a bizarre situation in triplicate.

I had to "entertain" Mr. Murphy, sing ditties like "Too Ra Loo Ra Loo Ra" like a pro and appear delighted at a chance to perform. Suspicions rattled me.

I didn't own a bathrobe. Never mind that my pajamas, a faded *Snow White* print weren't white anymore and way too big. "You'll grow into them," Mommy insisted about my few clothes, all oversized.

She must have believed that I'd grow wide, not tall. I always looked sloppy, unkempt. Once I fastened the droopy waistline of my one and only skirt, brand new, with a large safety pin. I camouflaged my baggy look with an oversized sweater. I never glanced in the mirror. I knew I looked repulsive. And there I was in my limp large pajamas facing a strange man.

Mommy didn't seem distrustful that the tipsy guest turned out to be one of Daddy's big shot political cronies with notable influence in the legal system, especially City Hall and the local divorce courts. My civics teacher spoke glowingly about him in class, deified him. He was a man of our neighborhood, one of us, working his way to the inner sanctums of Washington. D.C.

But I learned more than I wanted to know about Mr. Murphy.

"Murph," as Daddy called his pudgy pal, yielded legislative power.

I wish I'd never met him.

Mr. Murphy was a stealthy man who knew whom to reward for favors in courts of law. Mr. Murphy knew the ins and outs of the dissolution of a marriage and which partner could easily be shortchanged. Most especially, and this was the point of the dead-of- night gathering, this man knew how Daddy could get a full custodial warrant against Mommy, who sat there smiling.

Mommy was being hoaxed and hoodwinked.

Poor Mommy. And me? Would I be kidnapped?

Mr. Murphy, that's how I addressed him, could and would tip the scales in Daddy's favor for a handout, money plus liquor, and fine food, no charge, ad infinitum.

Mommy was obviously ignorant that we were the subjects of one of Daddy's most dangerous frauds. Truly, I have no idea how I came to all these grown-up conclusions. I did not "get" all this on my own. How could I possibly have figured out Daddy's underhanded strategy?

The 1,000 angels must have pooled their powers to force me, quickly and with unbelievable efficiency, to understand the profound basics of a bitter divorce. Daddy had local government friends, like Mr. Murphy, who had friends with friends. Daddy had at his disposal both means and men with means.

Mommy nudged me onto the piano seat.

I glanced at a beefy man who looked like a shabby Santa Claus out of costume. The 1,000 angels saw me as I was: a girl making music for the man who'd eventually become Speaker in a future White House. The perfect irony was that Mr. Murphy was, in essence, the speaker of our house, the house Mommy wanted to disband.

The man, *this* man, was Daddy's informal legal representative, his advisor, and Mommy's oncoming nemesis, the man who'd stop her, thwart her escape. My 1,000 angels told me to go along with Daddy's charade, recognize it for what it was: a dangerous parody.

Mommy still smiled happily, totally unaware of the manacles Daddy's guest held, the manacles which were the size of her slim wrists.

She thought I was a tiny talent show and that Daddy was showing me off. Her smile was the smile of a mother's pride.

I played and sang Irish ditties. I played as if I wasn't made aware of Daddy's motives. I played as if I wasn't wearing raggedy pajamas, as if my feet weren't cold and bare and that I had to sit at the very edge of the piano stool to reach the pedals. I did not own slippers. I played it the way my 1,000 angels told me to play it. Convincingly.

Mr. Murphy clapped in delight. He asked for encores. I played on.

Later, dozy but unable to sleep, I overheard Daddy berating Mommy with a slew of burn words.

In an instant, I was wide-awake.

It dawned on me that what I was hearing was the awful, awful "truth" forecast by my 1,000 angels. Something, or someone, pushed me into the sitting position. Sitting up ramrod straight I heard the "truth." It reeked of tragedy. It centered on me. Kidnapping! I understood that I was going to be kidnapped. This was no longer a shadowy threat. It was reality.

"Murph," Daddy proclaimed, would be the first politician that he'd access to stop any court proceeding my mother might initiate, even if she sought only legal separation.

"*She*, the dumbbell," Daddy said, referring to the absent me, "will be taken from you."

Daddy destructions were like Tasers, unexpected and efficient. I knew Mommy was shaking. She always shuddered when Daddy told her how useless her divorce ambitions were. He reminded her, sarcasm dripping from his voice, that they were "chained together."

"Tonight," he proclaimed, "I brought home a powerful politician, to show you that you have no marital or familial rights." He hesitated for a split second, then hammered home his ultimatum. "Murph will be my ally in and out of the courts. You're going to lose the dumbbell."

I imagined him looking at Mommy with his usual contempt.

"You're fighting a one-woman war," he chuckled with a lingering mockery that had the impact of a backhanded slap.

Mommy laughed.

It was a hysterical laugh, high-pitched, unnatural, and it lasted too long.

This was how her collapses began. She threw her head back and laughed at the tragedy facing her. She became a temporary second-rate actress, pretending that she wasn't overwrought, pretending that Daddy's stark threats, horrible and true, weren't a formal declaration of war.

This musical evening had tragedy written all over it.

I knew Mommy composed herself by folding her hands in her lap. That's what she always did. That's how she fabricated calm. I didn't hear Mommy's questions. She must have spoken in a tone as flat as she felt.

She must have asked Daddy where he'd take me if she left him, where would I go? I heard his terrifying answer. "I'll give the dumbbell to one of my sisters. I'll have her kidnapped. You'll never know which sister has her. You'll never know where I'll move them."

He repeated the bleak remains of her future.

Penniless. Homeless. Friendless. Condemned. Her baby kidnapped, gone.

Daddy's five childless sisters, a band of bossy female desperados, were Mommy's sworn enemies. They harassed this house divided. Singly, they were disgustingly condescending. As a group, they rallied against her like a battalion of armed executioners bent on destroying her.

Mommy exuded cover girl glamour.

They wore printed housedresses, chef's aprons, and mannish shoes that added to their unattractiveness. They had no babies. Daddy promised he'd do his best to hand me, his baby, over to them.

They hosted family dinners and gave Mommy the wrong address. When we got to that address, no one was home. We had no idea which sister-in-law was the party-giver. That's how they told us we weren't welcome within their scope of acceptance. We, as a unit, were nothing.

Me? That was a whole other issue. They wanted me in their fold. Me!

The five sisters always remained Mommy's most malicious critics.

They envied Mommy's radiance, her natural sense of chic, the erect way she walked in high heels They hated what they guessed was her hold on their only brother and his "connections," as Daddy called his team of chauvinist boozers. Daddy bought his political favors like he bought his church blessings, with fat checks.

That night, after the Irish music concert ended and Mr. Murphy was sent home in a pre-paid taxi, Daddy also ranted about church.

"Whichever sister gets her will take her to *my* church," Daddy bragged. "She'll become one of us."

Daddy knew exactly how to kill Mommy's natural feelings of delight in me. I heard the cruelty written in his voice. It sounded like a distant echo of a marital tumult rooted in something I still couldn't identify. In the process of destroying Mommy, he was killing me.

Now, overhearing Daddy's clearly stated power position, his flawless strategies, I wished I were dead. I was the cause of Mommy's despair, her anguish. We were both imprisoned in Daddy's crooked lifestyle. I had a habit of freezing into an unnatural stillness when Mommy was under fire.

I simply froze in my warm shabby bed, which turned cold.

Mommy's religion wasn't Daddy's religion. Mommy told Daddy he could *take me to his church on his own, without her. That was trouble. The only* connection Daddy had to his church was as a financial benefactor. He wanted to force Mommy to take me to his church or, as he loftily put it, "my church is *the* church."

She had always refused.

When it came to her religion, Mommy had a stubborn streak.

Every Sunday, I went to church with Mommy. I had a small cardboard collection box. I filled it with pennies, found on the street and earned, and put them into the collection plate. In an isolated room at the back end of the church, I babysat boisterous children who couldn't be trusted to be quiet during the service.

I told them stories about crocodiles, a little black dog called Teddy, and rocky caves in the sky. When they asked for more, I told then that I'd seen a white glob that turned into 1,000 angels that didn't look like angels. The Reverend told Mommy that I was an "exceptional" storyteller.

When Daddy finished the church tirade, he returned to kidnapping.

"You'll never see the dumbbell again," were Daddy's final words to her.

I felt Mommy's suffering, this awful bullying, so acutely and, so deeply, that I thought Daddy's plans were mightier than God's.

I didn't hear God. I heard Daddy.

His musical tactic, with me as the focus, seemed so precise, so well-timed, so plausible and potentially more terrible than anything Mommy or I ever guessed. It wasn't only the sisters-in-law who eagle-eyed me, wanted to take me away from her. It was Daddy and his powerful aides, men like Mr. Murphy.

I loved Mommy. I thought she loved me. Now I knew she loved me more than I thought. She stayed married to Daddy, who was driving her mad, in order to hold onto me.

The awful truth, now so painfully clear, was centered on me.

I was the culprit, the transgressor, and the source of Mommy's anguish.

I was her biggest burden, the daughter who stood in the way of her redemption from Church, from Daddy, from life.

I was everything Mommy wanted and nothing she wanted.

I was the greatest contradiction of her life.

She loved me, and she didn't.

I wanted to yip and yell until I was hoarse.

The night I played Irish ditties, I discovered my own dismal reality. I stood in Mommy's way. I was her biggest stumbling block! Mommy loved me enough to stay with Daddy so she could have me around her.

How could she love me under these ghastly circumstances?

A bullet shot through my heart! She loved me enough not only to stay, to be my protector. She sacrificed herself to a horrible marriage to save me It was costing her sanity! She was torn apart! That's why she was so shaky, so rash.,

It was entirely my fault. I was Mommy's abomination!

Chapter Fifteen
Dreaming

I fell into a restless sleep. I had a dream that didn't seem like a dream.

My 1,000 angels knocked a bolt of electricity through me that didn't burn. It warmed me up, got me tightly focused on the white circle circling round and round over my bed. I stared at it too long. It hypnotized me again.

A huge billboard rose out of what appeared to be a giant cloud of mist.

The angels staged liaisons with me in ways that defied human imagination. They didn't write letters. Typewriters, never mind computers, were not in their toolbox. Angels spoke without speaking. They could communicate on musical notes. They had other odd resources, their own uncommon languages.

I told myself to accept their latest marvel, to go with the flow.

The first billboard transfixed me. "Turn things around."

When the message sunk in, when I realized that the angels helped those who helped themselves, the billboard went pouf, became part of the atmosphere.

The next billboard was wordier, more specific.

"When you're alone, stuck in silence, you aren't really alone. You can hear yourself think. You can hear us reaching out to you."

It was true. The angels knew that I held everyone and everything in deep distrust except them.

"Suspicion is a synonym for uncertainty," read the next billboard. "If you doubt yourself, you'll achieve nothing."

No one being, much less a mass of supernatural beings, had ever treated me with such civility. Respect, or any kind of admiration, was unknown to me. I didn't even have a scrap of self-esteem. The angels respected my intelligence.

A new billboard was lowered.

"Fear of change is what imprisons you," it read.

I went haywire. This was too personal. This was too much interference. I was angry. I whimpered. I thought, *how does a weakling dumbbell initiate change when she is cuffed by unconscionable rules of silence and serfdom.* Emotionally disabled girls who happen to be petite and pathetic do not have the ability, or means, to change what cannot be changed. Those negative thoughts swallowed me.

The angels ignored my inaudible outburst.

They retained their civility.

They clarified the billboard message.

"We meant only that you should turn around the *idea* of being stuck forever behind an impenetrable wall."

I don't know how the angels controlled my misgivings, my sarcasm, and replaced the sinister negatives chomping on my insides with a balm that ultimately became known, in the real world, as the power of positive thinking.

Daddy didn't control my mind. *I did.*

I breathed three deep Yoga sighs. Relief clutched me.

Another billboard plopped into view.

"You didn't have to play deaf. You were never alone.

We saw what was happening."

I was in a fairy tale, an alien place, baffled by billboards that slid into my consciousness from nowhere, talking to forces I didn't know existed and, honestly, I was feeling good.

"The rawness of your emotions makes you super-sensitive," the next billboard proclaimed.

Then another: "You feel things more deeply, more fervently than ordinary people. These are the makings of an artist."

Without warning the highway signs puffed away, disintegrated, became air. I had gotten all my messages.

The circling shiny white ball reappeared.

It talked. I don't know how it talked. All I know is that I heard talk.

"In the future, when you write a story or paint a story, your sensitivity will be one of your best tools."

The angels lifted me up and away. I know this sounds funny but they had the same effect as getting my tonsils removed. I resisted a tight clamp on my face. Too many strong hands held me down on a hard steel table covered only in a white sheet. I went limp. The ether took me gliding, drifting, dreaming, believing in wonderlands.

The voice, or voices, returned.

"We're made of steel," said a voice only I heard. "No one can disband us. We're invisible to all but you. And we will always be aggressive on your behalf."

Then the glob dematerialized.

I woke up in my narrow bed, under the old quilts, in the old house to my old life.

Chapter Sixteen
Defiance

Where were the angels when I needed their benediction?

I'd just emerged from a Daddy chaos. He'd been on a rampage. He happened upon a library book about the art of writing. I'd hidden it in a kitchen cupboard, behind bashed pots and pans, but that was not good enough.

Daddy was always looking through bureau drawers, cabinets, and pantries. He thought of them as hiding places. In this case, he was right. I was taken to task as his words lashed at me like a whip in motion.

"Don't ever defy me, dumbbell," he'd threatened when he caught a glint of rebellion, a fast flash of defiance, spring into my eyes. I detested his tirades. I scorned his brainwashing techniques. I disdained being his prisoner. I don't know how I stood still as a statue when such fire swept through me.

"Do you know that creativity, however expressed, even in a spoken idea, is not within a woman's realm?"   he growled.

I gave Daddy, the lord of all I surveyed, what he wanted: silence.

He nodded disdainfully.

"Female intelligence is the stuff of showoffs," he sneered. "It's disrespectful to men. Remember that, dumbbell."

When Daddy called me dumbbell, he really meant it. I overheard him tell Mommy that I was "thick-headed" and "just plain stupid."

"Do you accept that you are a dummy?" he'd asked me earlier that day, for no reason. Daddy corrupted his favorite word, dumbbell, by making it sound slangy and cheap. He always wanted me to feel totally unwanted.

I said nothing. He thought my silence meant that I accepted being his dummy. He was so satisfied with my obedience that he nodded and marched off. I was always glad to see him go.

I quaked under Daddy's absolute authority. He controlled my physical comings and goings. His commandment of silence still traumatized me. But he did not control my imagination.

He didn't know how adept I'd become at bolting to my on-high cave.

All it took was a blink, and I found myself sitting outside the cave's opening overlooking a beautiful seascape with an endless horizon. It was there that I wrote stories in words and drew images that were stories without words.

I needed to know more about the soul.

What really goes on in there?

I knew I was repressed. Mommy was repressed. Were all men like Daddy, extreme chauvinists? Were all men ultimate controllers? I was without ammunition. There was no way I, a dumbbell girl, could fight a male oppressor.

The angels interrupted. "Forget dumbbell," they chimed again. I'd heard that often.

That's when I began to think beyond my "dumbbell"

tag.

What I thought then, sitting on my on-high cave, was that Mommy and I weren't the only females treated as if we were subservient to men, unequal to men in intellect, objectivity and, most of all, talent.

I must be part of a vast army, a nation, of pre-Feminist women who fought battles behind closed doors that were really the homes of the brave.

I was nearly twelve years old. I already knew what it was to be mocked, degraded, cursed, and ignored on the basis of my gender. I was home schooled on the horrific meaning of dysfunction. Were my 1,000 angels a symbol, a forecast, even a promise that one day all these dumbbell memories would be erased?

I wonder… I wonder.

It was there, in the on-high cave that a butterfly landed on my nose and looked me straight in the eye.

I touched my nose.

There was nothing there.

Chapter Seventeen
The Church Man

Mommy, in desperate straits, had a gambling streak. She decided to make a last-ditch effort or, as she murmured to herself: "I'm going to put all my cards on the table."

There was no money for either marriage counseling or a psychiatrist. The Reverend, any caring Reverend available was, hopefully, her only potential ally and trusted confidante.

She telephoned the Church office and asked to speak privately to a staff clergyman. Her marriage was messy. She wanted to talk things out, unburden herself. There was no fee, except for what Mommy put in the Sunday collection plate offering. An appointment was made.

Now, The Reverend, a stranger, was in the next room.

The kitchen sink was my territory. I stopped clanking the pile of dirty dishes and turned off the running faucet. I had to hear Mommy's marital confession intelligibly, in her own words. An adjacent door had been left ajar. Like a ghost in the shadows who was quiet as a mouse, I hid behind that door.

This snooping was justified. That's what I told myself.

Mommy and the Reverend were sitting opposite each other.

"I have made a terrible mistake," Mommy blurted out her first excruciating confession in total despair. Her voice broke. "My marriage is in shambles. I want a divorce."

The sad words, reeking regret, hung in the air between two people from two different worlds. Mommy tried to make direct eye contact with The Reverend. But his eyes were stuck on an endless stream of huge green ferns printed haphazardly across the cheap blue wallpaper of our tiny living room.

He was still eyeing the wallpaper when he asked: "And when did you realize you'd made a mistake?

Mommy was in dreadful need of emotional release. Her marriage was in total chaos. Despairing people like Mommy don't care if they're talking to someone who seems to be talking to the wall.

"Oh, I knew it right away," Mommy continued, ignoring the minister's patronization.

This was her last-ditch effort. She was a frustrated woman on a reckless journey toward freedom. She had to speak out, release her desperations or go insane. She didn't care if The Reverend heard her plea. He just had to listen, or even pretend to listen, to her pathetic articulation of wifedom with Daddy. She mistook, perhaps on purpose, the Reverend's condescension for his undivided attention.

I studied the Reverend. He was making Mommy nervous, shaky. I didn't like him. The Reverend's distant attitude was so chilly, so unreceptive that Mommy's excruciatingly private disclosures became increasingly discombobulated.

The Reverend, speaking low like a curt court interrogator, asked what she meant by "right away."

"What do you mean you mean when you said you knew you'd made a mistake right away?"

His tone was prosecutorial.

"As I was walking to the altar," she sputtered candidly,

sounding like a runaway bride who didn't run.

She continued breathlessly: "And before I said 'I do.'

She paused to take a deep breath.

"And when I walked down the aisle after the ceremony," she admitted ruefully.

"At my own wedding, I was in crisis, wishing I were somewhere else."

Her confession, stark and sorrowful, reached The Reverend's ears but not his heart. The Reverend asked what convinced her that the marriage would work when she was so overcome with pre-wedding doubts.

"Was this a case of the jitters?" he asked coolly.

"My marriage was a terrible mistake," she stammered. Her voice broke again. She recovered herself. Succinctly, slowly, and emphatically, she spilled again what was on her mind: "I want to end it."

Mommy surfed over important details. She was making this petition for help behind Daddy's back. She knew Daddy might walk in. Daddy had a habit of just appearing out of nowhere. That possibility made this moment even more crucial, more nerve-wracking.

But in the annals of her confused mind, she was trying to gather support that might sustain her during any future confrontations with Daddy's gang, especially the drunken Mr. Murphy and his crooked cronies. She was on thin ice. If Daddy found her with The Reverend now, sputtering her truths, it would be a catastrophe.

She sat stiffly expecting understanding where there was none.

Mommy had not told The Reverend that Daddy promised her a life of pure luxury, that he had only one precious thing in his possession at the time they met, that gold Montblanc pen, which he pressed into her hands, that he held for a long, long time, too long. Daddy told her this was only the beginning of a blissful moneyed life, a litany of precious gifts coming her way.

Mommy did not say that Daddy was deceptive about

his richness. He had no money to spend on new clothes, a new car, a new house, and high-class entertainment. She did not say to the Reverend: look around, does this neighborhood, this house, speak of wealth? I knew it was on the threshold of her tongue.

Instead, she groaned, "I've been duped."

Mommy needed consolation and, in a broader sense, absolution. She needed guidance and support. A churchman, someone who was trustworthy enough to hear her intimate secrets and keep them secret was, she thought, the person who'd tell her one big mistake wasn't final, that there was always a second chance.

But The Reverend's negativity vibrated its chilliness all the way to where I hid. He wasn't going to tell her what she wanted to hear.

Mommy made a split-second decision. She had to speak up, expose the whole dreary mess, or she'd explode. I could see that her urgent desire for release, an inner emotional cleansing, was far, far stronger than being discovered by Daddy and far, far stronger than the Reverend's obvious disinterest.

She persisted to tell her anguished story, hoping to get positive feedback.

"I was married late in January," she started over with more patience than I knew she had. "Within weeks, I was pregnant." She didn't tell The Reverend that she was not yet nineteen and yearned for couture clothes, real jewelry, exuberant parties. Mommy wanted to be wooed, courted, not inseminated.

"I didn't want that baby," she resounded. "I wasn't ready."

What? What? What?

I was the baby she didn't want?

I stumbled in shock. Mommy heard me waver. She knew I was listening behind the door. She wanted me to hear her brutal honesty in this roundabout way. She was telling me, through The Reverend, that I was a most unwelcome child. Mommy's idea of honesty was always connected to bluntness. That was her way.

This revelation stunned me. The night I was required to play Irish ditties for Mr. Murphy, the angels told me I would hear the truth. Part of the truth was missing that night. This was the whole blunt truth whizzing into me, trapping me, burning me.

"We'd known each other only a few weeks," Mommy was admitting candidly. "I expected our courtship to continue. That's what I was promised, more courtship. I got pregnant instead," she repeated. "It was a mistake."

Out of all the ridiculous romantic melodrama she was revealing, it all came down to her biggest mistake, me.

I was the mistake.

I crumbled inside.

Me! Oh my god, Mommy never wanted me. I came too soon when I shouldn't have come at all. My birth had blocked her lifestyle, her ambitions and, ultimately, her escape.

That's why, over the years, her resentment towards me had steadily escalated from protective to mercenary. Sharp pangs of remorse skewered me. Or was it contrition? I had been an unwanted baby. Now I was just plain unwanted. I'd been on the unhappy path since I'd popped into the world.

Much later in life, Mommy confided to me that Daddy didn't use condoms. He preferred a timely withdrawal.

Unfortunately, his timing was way off when he permeated her with me. When she confided this morsel, I suspected that Daddy didn't withdraw on purpose. He wanted a pregnant wife fast, a woman who wanted to change her lifestyle and her lipstick but was forced to change diapers instead. When she fell into Daddy's trap, I fell into hers.

Mommy started to speak again.

Her voice broke again.

She retrieved it.

"I did not want to be pregnant," she said vehemently.

"Everything about the marriage was a mistake."

She began to sound like a broken record repeating the same emotions in virtually the same words. What stopped her from presenting her case more logically was The Reverend's continued blatant indifference. She didn't say Daddy had planned on a shipboard affair and had landed a wife.

With one eye, I peeked around the door and got a good look at our visitor, an unmarried and uncaring man who had no sympathy for wives with revolting problems.

The Reverend, ageless, was a tall skinny man with a sandy crew cut. His imposing black suit had a starched white clergy dog collar that seemed to suffocate him. He was a human metaphor for unbendable church laws.

His attitude toward Mommy was clearly adversarial, like a lion waiting for the right moment to pounce. She made his stance easy. She kept on talking about "false pretenses" and the "unwanted pregnancy." She spoke like a wronged woman, not a clear-minded defender of her case. Emotionally abused people are not logical when they try to explain their straits. They're all mixed up. So is the scrambled way they talk. I was an awful lot like Mommy.

The courtship. She kept on going back to courtship.

She'd wanted a period of sustained romance, the feeling of being romantically pursued, the sureness of their complete compatibility. Daddy hadn't courted her long enough. She neither desired nor was she prepared for frequent serious sex

I couldn't believe Mommy was admitting such highly classified information to the now-squirming Reverend whose gaze had gotten even more icy. He was deliberately inattentive or, at least, appeared to be.

I listened hard. I'd gleaned a lot of information from romance novels hidden under my bed. I thought, *when they married, perhaps Daddy seduced her too quickly. Maybe he violated her. Maybe he forced her. Mommy was too young, too carefree to be burdened with a baby. She had surrendered to him too quickly. Surrender and love are not necessarily synonymous.*

When I was thinking these thoughts, Mommy repeated everything she'd already said. She was beautiful. She sat in the corner of a couch, in a demure navy blue dress with matching high heel pumps, her legs crossed at the ankle. She sat with her hands clasped to keep them still. She was anxious for intelligent responses, even a small condolence about her "mistake."

Mommy got nothing from The Reverend.

He did not acknowledge the profundity of her ramble.

He sat rigidly, maintaining his mask of maddening blankness. By now, the Reverend was completely closed off. She knew it. She was smart. But she was also emotionally wrought.

Once and for all, she had to get all this all out. A lackadaisical church minister was the best listener at her disposal. Only he didn't give a hoot. Her need to rid herself from bondage escalated, free what was left of her dwindling inhibitions. His disinterest was frosty.

"The marriage should not have been consummated so fast," she disclosed passionately, as if the mistake, *me*, had happened yesterday.

Without blaming Daddy further, she disclosed that the marriage could have been annulled quickly if she'd spoken up, or walked away.

I never knew that.

Mommy disclosed that her late uncle, an Anglican Bishop assigned to a cathedral in England, could have initiated an annulment easily if, big if, the marriage hadn't been consummated. Apparently, Daddy knew that. That's why he became an immediate, serious and insistent lover. Daddy played god better than God. Except when Daddy ordered a son, God decreed otherwise.

"It was one mistake after the other," Mommy was repeating bleakly. Even now, hearing her drab truth about being pregnant with me, I loved her honesty, her dignity, and most of all, the courage it took to expose the details of the intense sexual married life that began too soon. This was the match made in hell.

She hadn't fallen in love. She'd fallen for Daddy's con.

The Reverend's attitude toward Mommy became glacial.

"I didn't want that baby," she repeated, as if The Reverend, as if I, hadn't heard that admission, and other related admissions, too many times. "I wasn't ready."

Mommy's poignant reiterations were based on the belief that The Reverend was missing her valid points. She held on. The conversation, so one-sided, did not bring her the consolation she'd expected, desired and needed.

The Reverend did not probe.

He did not ask if Daddy was too aggressive or if too much sex was instigated too early in the marriage. Mommy had been a virgin. She had proof. She kept the stained sheet from the marriage bed tucked among her personal belongings. I found it after she died, folded perfectly, wrapped in blue tissue paper. The bloodstains had turned to rust.

She was trying to find a loophole in Daddy's threats, something on which to build hope of bolting out of the marriage.

"I cried every day for the whole nine months," she conceded guiltily. "I produced a daughter who is sad all the time."

The Reverend abstained from any comment about a pregnant woman's emotions being transmitted to the fetus, passed on to the newborn,

"I thought it was love," Mommy blurted. "He promised... he promised everything but a new fur coat every year. I believed him," she said and suddenly sobbed into one of Daddy's large initialed cotton handkerchiefs big enough to cover her face. I hadn't ironed it. She must have grabbed it from the ironing basket.

Mommy dried her tears. She had a few more revelations.

"He doesn't support us well. I can't make ends meet.

"He prohibits any pleasures, socializing of any type.

"He deprives his daughter of books.

"He calls his daughter a dumbbell," she cried. "He refers to her as 'She.' It's not her baptismal name."

When The Reverend heard about names that weren't proper names, he smirked surreptitiously. He couldn't have cared less.

What surprised me most was hearing her regrets about my emotional abuses. I thought she had already joined forces with Daddy, sanctioning his shabby treatment of me. Now, in the repentant way she talked to The Reverend, I thought she still had a semblance of motherly love for me. I thought that in her heart of hearts she was still an independent thinker.

I also knew that my presence was an irritant. I was a constant reminder of her mistake. How long would her just-expressed compassion for me last? Not long.

The Reverend was a strict ecclesiastic who did not deviate from ancient man-made Church canons. He didn't care about a romance gone horribly wrong. He certainly had no interest in the emotional abuse of women. He'd memorized pat answers to situations like Mommy's in Divinity School.

"I don't need to hear any more," is the way he dismissed her weeping, her blundered confession.

He was not going to help her.

"You knew all along," he chided, "that a marriage sanctioned by a formal church ceremony, with signed papers, amounts to a legal contract."

Mommy was being burned.

I felt her burn from where I was hiding.

Oh, I hate burns.

"When you were married in an official church ceremony, it was by the book," the Reverend solemnly declared pulpit-like, referring to the explicit religious wedding ceremony in The Book of Common Prayer.

He pulled the book, with a black cover, out of his little black briefcase, and waved it in her face. Even the news from the black clad man was black: "Your marriage is still legal and binding."

Mommy would have liked to play deaf like I used to play deaf. But she couldn't shut out the scathing words being rat-a-tatted into her ears. Legalese was The Reverend's reaction to the laying of all her cards on the table.

"The church, which I represent, cannot sanction your cause in any way whatsoever. You would be a divorcee. You would carry a stigma. A divorce is a disgrace, a terrible humiliation."

The Reverend, a bland man with an expressionless face, had been carefully schooled to ignore the depth of female anxieties, especially of the kind Mommy articulated. He was a pragmatist, a man of the cloth. Dogma was his business.

He brought up the word "love."

A flash of anger blazed through Mommy's brown eyes with long lashes that needed no mascara. "I don't love him now," Mommy retorted angrily. "And I didn't love him then."

She was at her most vulnerable, and she'd been talking to the wrong man. He increased her acute sense of defeat. I saw how her mouth drooped, how her body shrank. Mommy was on brink of collapse.

The Reverend tossed the main words of her contract back at her. "Besides love," he said, "you promised to honor and obey." He was pouring vinegar into her wounds, delivering the guilty verdict.

When he threw the words honor and obey at Mommy, I saw her shudder. There was no honor in their union. "How can a woman willingly obey a man whom she doesn't respect?" Mommy asked with such pathos, I wanted to weep too.

The Reverend had no answer except the book answer.

"You *must* honor and obey your husband. It's church law," he repeated with even more emphasis.

His words paralleled what Mommy heard from Daddy too often: "It's your duty." Now this man was killing her identically, and he had an imposing edifice backing him, The Church.

Mommy held in her grief.

The Reverend reminded Mommy that she was married in church, in front of God and guests and, thus, there were "witnesses." He stated, clearly, that she was bound to this man when she accepted, of her own volition, the horrible phrase, "till death do us part."

The Reverend had articulated every dreaded injunction Mommy knew. She was seeking empathy, even redemption, and this strange interloper, an intruder representing the crucifix, had slammed every door in her face.

When she was painted into a corner unable to move forward, when she realized the uselessness of her call for help, she deflected to humor.

"You mean I've made my bed, and I have to sleep in it," she said from a forced smile. Her comment had a double meaning. Mommy had great wit she rarely showed in Daddy's presence. In this situation, her wit gave her closure.

The Reverend nodded. I did not hear his voice. I heard him leaving. I heard Mommy thank him for coming. This was the polite side of her, the ladylike charm of standing tall when she'd just been cut down.

I slunk *back* to my sink job. The dishes clashed loudly. I banged them around. The inner me clashed even more loudly.

An abrupt and pathetic shriek of frustration crashed through the walls and split my eardrums. The sound was so shattering, so deep-rooted that I knew it emanated from Mommy's gut, not her throat.

She'd lost the battle, the war, and her freedom. She was alone in her bedroom. She was alone everywhere, anywhere. At that moment, she wanted to scream alone, separate herself from me.

Especially from me.

Chapter Eighteen
Screams

Much later, I saw Edward Munch's pre-expressionist painting, "The Scream," and I imagined Mommy's face superimposed on the face of the screamer. I remembered how I'd knocked on her door, and there was no answer. I wanted to scream too.

I was overcome with shame that I'd been born too soon. Worse, I shouldn't have made my way to this planet. I should have been aborted. Mommy had told the Reverend, clearly, if she hadn't been pregnant with me, she could have pursued another life.

I still have their wedding photo.

Mommy wore a flowing white dress designed by Nina Ricci in Paris. It was fashioned from Chantilly lace. The weightless chiffon veil sprouted from a halo. Her long, silky chestnut hair was pulled back into a sleek French twist. She seemed so delicate, so shy, so unsure of what she'd done. Question marks filled her eyes where unshed tears lurked. I knew they were not tears of happiness.

Daddy stood militarily, like a proud general in a tuxedo. He was then what he was now: a commando bent on dictatorship. I think Mommy sensed that her groom was a tyrant in disguise but didn't want to believe it. "Pre-marital jitters," she was told.

These were pre-Feminist times. Women had no rights. They were millions of homebodies and nobodies under mass duress. They were the brave women who had to find ways to get their way in small ways.

They were just like Mommy.

Once when Daddy was on his way to the drug store, she slipped a folded piece of paper in the pocket of his jacket. "It's a list of things I need," she'd smiled. Daddy thought they were medicinal. The druggist collected the items, put them in a bag, and gave Daddy the bill for an entire collection of the newest Max Factor cosmetics.

Daddy, shocked he'd been tricked, had a reputation for generosity to protect. He paid up. It was close to Thanksgiving. We ate cereal on that holiday. Daddy ate a lavish turkey dinner at his restaurant. That was our punishment.

Mommy got her driver's license behind Daddy's back.

That was a big deal with big repercussions. He withheld the small household budget for weeks. We lived on bread and green olives stuffed with pimento. We made a small jar last a long time. Mommy and I smiled at each other, pretending not to care.

She wanted liberty more than food. I wanted Mommy more than Daddy.

Later she even convinced him to buy her a second-hand car.

I took it all in, everything. I would never get married. I would never call a child a mistake. If I ever loved a man, I'd agree to a relationship, not a ring.

I wanted no ties that bind except, of course, books and paints.

Chapter Nineteen
Laundry

Serious suitors, not only hustlers, made inquiries about the state of Mommy's murky marriage. Neighborhood busybodies, a bunch of closet spies, knew too much, saw too much, and, if a little bribe was involved, gossiped too much.

Daddy came under their scrutiny too. Despite his image of extravagant church benefactor, the neighbors twittered how he, or any man in his right mind, failed to put a woman like Mommy on a pedestal?

Everyone knew that Mommy had become emotionally delicate. Her severely injured ego needed bolstering. I'd watched her test what was left of her female prowess with a playful expertise that I admired.

Mommy's flirting was so dignified that it appeared to be sincere friendliness. She had conspicuous curves and walked pencil-straight, head up. Men who happened to cross her path ogled her graceful stride with its suave little skip. Then they checked out her face, sculpted and smooth. Many men found her irresistible. If a man got too bold, she showed him her wedding ring.

Daddy hadn't been around for days. He frequently disappeared into thin air.

Mommy relaxed.

Her manners were polished, and so were her manicured nails, stroked in deep red. She was always fashionably dressed, chic clothes she'd made herself. Mommy looked like a movie star.

Minutes before the doorbell rang, she'd been singing Disney songs accompanying herself on the piano. She'd stopped abruptly, went blank. Lingering thoughts of the combined power of Mr. Murphy, the politician, and The Reverend from Church, loitered in her brain, slowed her thoughts.

When the worst memories rose, she simply stopped dead in her tracks. She'd be talking and suddenly freeze. Or she'd be in the kitchen chopping vegetables, and stop to stare inwardly. Or somebody would talk to her, expecting a response, and she'd just clam up.

I was within earshot when she'd been warbling that famous Disney song, "Someday My Prince Will Come." Instead of singing the specific lyrics, the actual title phrase, she substituted her own peculiar prognostication: "And no more princes for me"

That summarized her state of mind.

But there he was, a blond Viking god, Daddy's polar opposite, ringing the doorbell unexpectedly, on an ordinary day, and good luck fell from nowhere and landed in Mommy's handshake.

I was the girl who was never heard, much less seen. I concealed myself by rolling into the thick folds of faded castoff brocade drapes, discards from one of Daddy's restaurants. Luckily my eye level peephole was an actual gouge in the fabric.

The tall, stately man with an aristocratic aura exuded importance. He'd parked in front of our house. His automobile was a chauffeured Cadillac, glossy black, with spotless whitewall tires and a red leather interior. Both the automobile and its owner were painfully out of place in our cheap, lower class neighborhood.

With an outstretched hand to Mommy, the man introduced himself.

When he caught sight of Mommy's impeccable manicure, which she'd done herself, fascination snapped into his glittering eyes. Mommy's hands were graceful, her fingers long and soft. Then his eyes swept over her swiftly. Everything about her echoed a sexy glow.

The smitten man was a high-priced divorce lawyer who tried big cases and was eagle-eyed by newspaper photographers who trained their long-range lens on him when he wasn't nearby. I'd seen front-page newspaper photos of him strolling down the courthouse steps, English-style leather briefcase in hand, looking like the cinema version of a legal superstar in a custom double-breasted pinstripe suit.

He told Mommy he'd come to our house to have Daddy sign papers. Daddy wasn't home. The lawyer admitted that he'd already stopped by the restaurant. Daddy wasn't there either.

The lawyer smiled at Mommy in a steadfast way and divulged the truth. He'd come to the house on a serious whim. "There are no coincidences," he said quickly when Mommy squirmed slightly, "only perfect timing."

He'd planned this meeting, making it appear innocent and extemporaneous, knowing Daddy's exact whereabouts at that time. He was the kind of polished legal professional who knew precisely how to sidestep a potential triangle. Mommy had an ardent admirer. He sat sitting opposite her, his velvet-collared gray Chesterfield coat still on, his gaze set on her gorgeous face.

This lawyer, like all men in Daddy's inner circle or even on his outer periphery, knew that this marriage was on the rocks. He was checking out Mommy up close, savoring the exquisite details of her. He liked what he saw. His bright blue eyes, like sparkling sapphires, gleamed with pleasure.

Those penetrating eyes also roamed and assessed the small shabby house, studded with meager furniture, and, finally, settled again on Mommy, a lovelorn indigent who had married down.

He seemed familiar with her inner insecurities. It was as if they were visible. He'd counseled broken-hearted clients before. In an instant, his eyes embraced Mommy with a heartfelt combination of passion-compassion the likes of which I'd never seen.

Was this what love-at-first-sight looked like?

Was instant love really so sincere, so consequential, so mesmerizing?

Or had this man already glimpsed Mommy many times on our walks to window shop in the nearby square? Maybe he'd studied her often from the backseat of his fancy automobile and, in one passing glance or, perhaps many, was overpowered by the delightful distraction of her youth and radiance.

Together they seemed so satisfied, so immersed in each other. How could this be?

He was a man openly enraptured. He stared at Mommy adoringly, as if he couldn't get enough of her. Mommy's eyes glinted with gladness. She was aware that she sat with a suitor.

And I readily thought to myself: this was what Mommy told The Reverend she craved, courtship. Only she was a married woman. The handsome man in our house beginning to pursue her seemed to know all about Daddy. It didn't stop him. He gazed at Mommy more tenderly, more adoringly, than Daddy ever did.

Mommy had needs. Communicating with an attractive man without stress was one of the most basic. Besides, a romantic link seemed to be blossoming.

The lawyer knew more about this sour marriage than he let on. He wanted to know little things about her, things that were part of her pre-Daddy life. He seemed to know everything else.

"Tell me all about you," he sighed, his voice trailing. "You."

His voice was soothing and steady. His attitude was solicitous and welcoming. Mommy responded by talking to him so openly, so uninhibitedly, with such a natural girlishness, it was if they'd known each other in some other life.

Mommy was transfixed by the man's fervent focus on her.

It was worship.

She'd always wanted to be worshipped by a man of consequence.

That was the Mommy I didn't know existed. That must be the glamorous, companionable Mommy that Daddy met on the cruise ship.

Still, I couldn't help but think that the timing with the amorous lawyer was wrong, that it was too late. Daddy, dangerous Daddy, was smack in the picture now. He acted as if he owned Mommy. She had a resume, one Daddy had tried to diminish and destroy, but it surfaced under the gaze of a man transfixed on her.

Mommy spoke modestly, in a dulcet voice. She told the lawyer that she was fluent in English, Spanish and Arabic. Her late father had been a global travel agency executive who launched new offices in major cities around the world. They'd lived in Cuba briefly and she'd been enrolled in a private girl's school in Havana. Her grades in that school, in all the schools she'd attended everywhere, were high.

"Except for gymnastics," Mommy grinned. Her teeth were pearly white and even. "I was never good at sports."

The lawyer nodded pleasantly. He was enthralled. She, a feminine woman, was under his most solicitous scrutiny. Mommy continued talking uninhibitedly. She basked in his open admiration. I'd never seen her like this. She was under his spell.

When her parents returned to their hometown Raleigh, North Carolina, her father's chauffeur taught her how to drive. She loved mathematics. Even though she was a lot younger than her classmates, she'd been a star student and graduated from the city's then-famous Kings Business College. She told the lawyer man that she treasured her diploma and, if she'd pursued a career, it would have been in high-level banking in a cosmopolitan city like New York, probably on Wall Street.

I'd never heard any of this before either.

She started to talk about cruise ships.

She stopped so abruptly, so clumsily, that the man leaned toward her, moved closer to comfort her. He mistook her sudden retreat into herself as a primal need to be kissed. He wanted to kiss Mommy impetuously, ardently.

From my secret vantage, that ridiculous peephole, I'd watched in fascination how a man approaches a woman romantically. It seemed to happen in slow motion. I saw a man and a woman drown in each other's gaze. Neither moved. Each looked at the other as if this connection, a powerful attraction, had to last a lifetime.

His face inched closer to hers. Mommy didn't hesitate. Her face was inches from his. That's when the love-at-first-sight ramifications hit me, excited me, electrified my imagination.

Oh boy! Oh boy!

This could be my new Daddy. I bet this Daddy, who looked as if he was headed for a court appearance, would let me write and paint and have as many books as my heart desired. I'd like to ride with him in his shiny cocoon set on whitewall tires that were white-white.

If escape was ever our possibility, this was the man. He had an athletic build. I envisioned him playing tennis on a country club court. I would like to learn how to play tennis. Even from where I hid, I got a whiff of his favorite scent, patchouli.

He'd never taken off his deftly tailored Burberry coat.

But I noticed that his navy silk tie was knotted the Windsor way, thickly, that his flannel trousers were sharply creased, and that his wingtip shoes were so shiny and smooth they looked new. Even his fingernails were neatly clipped. His hands were long and strong, not pudgy like Daddy's.

He was the epitome of a handsome hero, an impeccable prince, pursuing his heroine.

He made his first move.

Mommy's hands were folded. He reached out and put his hands over hers, a gesture of protection and desire. He asked Mommy if she wanted anything, needed anything, anything at all.

She shook her head, no.

Her eyes said yes. He heard yes.

That's when he blurted what was on his mind, in his heart, what had brought him here on false pretenses, those non-existent papers for Daddy to authorize.

"I would do anything for you," he said lovingly and meant it. The man spoke of whisking her away, buying her a big house somewhere new, getting her *anything* she wanted. "Anything," he said again. His voice underlined the word with an honorable pledge that even I, an innocent girl, understood was sincere.

Mommy didn't take her hands from under his.

He declared his intentions in a mellow voice as smooth as Devonshire cream. He said he knew how to get her a divorce, how to get her custody of me, how to keep Daddy and his cronies at bay. She had nothing to fear.

How did he know so much about Daddy's gang? This was no idle proposition. These were promises. I liked this potential Daddy. He had done his research. He came prepared. He could teach me how to organize my thoughts and state my case, whatever it happened to be. He wouldn't keep me silent. He'd teach me logic.

If he knew I was nearby, hidden in the drapes, maybe he would have asked me what I thought about the three of us starting a new life. I so wanted to be included in a regular family. This man was talking about normality.

Mommy's eyes fluttered in fear mixed with clear consent.

The lawyer man told Mommy not to be afraid. He assured her he knew precisely how to make things right in a court of law. His specialty was divorce. He had a team of experts to back him up. His crew would be her crew.

My heart was pumping with joy.

Escape!

This was Mommy's second chance, my second chance.

"Marry me!" the man implored. His eyes shone with love for Mommy, lust too. This man knew she had married down, He saw himself as her rescuer, her lover, her husband.

He repeated the proposal with an even greater confidence born of zeal; "Marry me. I've loved you from a distance for a long, long time." His face glowed with anticipation. He did not release his clasp of her hands. "Now I'm loving you up close."

If he had a diamond ring in his briefcase, maybe he did, he would have gone down on his knees.

Mommy said nothing. Her hands were still in his hands, not on top of one another, but entwined. She was stalling. I could tell.

Her hesitation, charming at first, turned into mild indifference. Oh, this was not a good sign. My heart sank. I wanted him to be my Daddy. I fidgeted inside the drapes waiting for Mommy to succumb. She wasn't succumbing.

I read Mommy's mind. She was comparing Daddy's old promises with the lawyer's new promises. They paralleled one another. It was eerie.

Daddy had probably made similar promises on a luxury cruise ship. They were all counterfeit. He, too, held her hands when he gave her his pen and pledged that his riches would be her riches.

What she was saddled with now were endless humiliations, denials of the basic necessities, everlasting spitefulness, a suspicion of adultery, and serious threats of kidnapping. It had all started romantically on a luxury cruise ship with two people holding hands, a man making promises to a woman.

Mommy had fallen for a con man, Daddy.

Now, look at us!

I know she had a fundamental urge to believe this man, run away with him, be with him, but she was scared out of her wits. Mommy had been burned. Oh, I hated burns. Mommy had already begun to believe that, in the final analysis, all men were like Daddy. Promises weren't promises. They were approaches, fraudulent ones.

She believed this man but not enough for her to get up and leave with him.

Daddy had duped her. Maybe the lawyer, with whom she was sharing an intense reaction, might be a replica of the man she'd married.

Daddy had changed her. Her natural daringness and her great sense of adventure had deserted her completely. Still, she couldn't help herself. She was obviously drawn physically and mentally to the lawyer. The two of them continued to hold hands.

This was still a courtship in progress.

Mommy visualized her sudden suitor as a propitious lover and husband. But what if his promises weren't real? His proposal was spur of the moment. Impromptu. He was a stranger. She'd taken a chance on Daddy, a stranger and fellow passenger on a cruise ship. She'd learned a lesson.

As I watched them from my peephole, I wondered if Mommy would ever take a chance on a man again.

She feared Daddy and his cronies. She feared Mr. Murphy's legal powers. She feared the Reverend's Church powers. She feared involving herself with divorce courts, with public accusations, and the snares of cross-examinations.

She wasn't strong enough then. She knew she could love this man. But she was too emotionally unsteady, too distraught, to handle Daddy's perilous fits, and all the evil a move of this magnitude could stir in him.

Mommy got too still, too unyielding, too quiet.

Her mind closed.

She shut down.

She'd been brainwashed, like me. When she'd smiled and told The Reverend that her bed was made and now she had to sleep in it, she meant it.

I looked at the man proposing to her, professing his desires. He had the authority, stride, and sureness of the prototype Princeton or Yale man. He had an impeccable side-part haircut and the sharp blue eyes of a classic Yankee Ivy Leaguer. Everything about him mirrored Hollywood matinee idol. He was also a high-priced Boston lawyer with clout.

He gazed at Mommy with an honest longing. He sensed that Mommy was slipping away from him. She was holding back. He was a man who'd been trained to scrutinize subtleties, interpret them. He realized that he wouldn't, or couldn't, have the woman he loved. A cloud crossed his face.

He knew of Mommy's emotional horrors. He'd had Daddy investigated thoroughly. He understood the specific causes of Mommy's depression. He believed he could remove them, make her happy.

He pressed on the way good lawyers do even when they're losing.

The clasped hands still did not unclasp. He was still courting her, telling her everything she had once wanted to hear. He never gave up in court. He would not give up on courting Mommy.

"Pack a suitcase," he urged. "Get your coat. Get your daughter. You don't need anything else. I am here for you. That's all you need." There was urgency in his voice. "We can leave now," he said impetuously.

He'd flung great pledges at Mommy, huge ones that had scope and life-changing meaning. He still wore his coat. I realized he hadn't taken it off because he was in a hurry to leave with us in tow immediately, then and there, no second thoughts.

Mommy listened hard.

His driver would take her, and me, to an unknown destination, one Daddy couldn't find. Even if the neighbors saw her leave, he assured her any insinuation of desertion would be thrown out in a court of law.

He told her he'd be her protector. Daddy was an emotionally abusive man. He knew the laws about "marital maltreatment" and would prove Daddy's abuse to a judge. He knew how to safeguard her and me.

Mommy was being lavished with the most endearing words of true devotion. She didn't stop him. Even if they never became a couple, she had to hear everything he said, all the promises, all the dreams. She had to remember this auspicious moment.

He spoke of her right to happiness. He was a widower with no children. He owned a city condominium high the sky, and a sprawling beach house overlooking a sea where the horizon stretched far. They were hers. I would be hers. A new house, with the proper help, would be hers. He'd have it built to her specifications.

His proposal was more real, more dedicated, and more generous than any woman as tangled as Mommy had a right to expect.

Say the word, he implored. "Marry me. We'll wait until everything is settled, and we'll have a lovely ceremony. " His face was still close to hers. He wanted to seal the deal with a romantic kiss. He leaned in. I could see that Mommy desired to fall into his arms, kiss him back.

But she didn't.

The lawyer's generous offer, far more honest than Daddy's blatant lies, was everything she'd ever wanted. Why should she turn it down? While she was considering the proposal she faded somewhere unreachable.

Even when Daddy wasn't in the room, the phantom of him always triumphed.

Long ago, when she'd finished chasing fortunetellers, Mommy mumbled to me: "I know what my fate is. I can't change it." She was referring to her wedding vows, bonds based on 16th-century laws that favored men. "Those whom God has joined, let no man put asunder," the Reverend had quoted the church's criterion.

This man of the cloth reminded her of the many binding agreements she'd made. He'd riddled her with guilt and shame. Daddy, using Mr. Murphy, had crushed most of her will to seek a legal separation. She'd been throttled by a double whammy.

Once, when she was in a blue mood, I told her that a court decision, divorce, was far better and more lasting than a church edict that did no good when a marriage was no good. That was when her hands had begun to shake uncontrollably, when Parkinson's began its initial cripple.

She was convinced there was no escaping Daddy. He'd terrorized us both. Daddy would murder her, have me kidnapped, given to one of the aunts. This man, this beautiful man proposing to Mommy, couldn't save us from the drastic calamities Daddy had strewn in our path.

I held my breath. I wanted to interfere, but I didn't dare. I wanted Mommy to play the proposal like she played Poker: to win. All she had to do is say yes. Or at least take time to think about saying "yes."

The lawyer, exuding nobility, held his breath. He too waited to hear "yes."

"Well, yes," Mommy smiled timidly. "I would like to have a new wooden drying stand for wet laundry."

The lawyer man was stupefied.

He paled and got choked up.

I, who was in charge of the wet laundry, was more stupefied. I did not want or need a new drying stand. I wanted to call this wonderful man Daddy and mean it. He had included me in the divorce strategy, in the settlement, in their marriage.

Mommy's imaginative answer was so ridiculous, so

absurd and so preposterous that, for an instant, I laughed inside just before tears of distress puddled down my cheeks.

Still standing lamely and lonely in the dusty old drapes, I peeked again at the lawyer man. He was beyond forlorn. Mommy had daggered his heart, He'd just lost the most important case of his personal life. Before releasing Mommy's hands, he squeezed them lovingly with an energy generated by intense desire. It was, in essence, a sad farewell.

The man was a true aristocrat. He was a solicitor who knew when to stop soliciting. He was the sophisticated gentleman Daddy never would be. He'd been professionally trained to read between the lines, gather clues, be a detective, assemble evidence and, after putting them together, face the facts.

He wanted Mommy. But he understood and empathized with her reticence. She pulled back. He knew that her abysmal fear of Daddy controlled her.

He kissed her hand. He kissed both her cheeks. He kissed her forehead. He kissed the top of her head. He looked longingly at her lips, hesitated, walked briskly out the door, climbed into his black car, which, in turn, flew him away.

The stand arrived the next day by special messenger. No card. It was a humble gift rich in what-might-have-been sentiment.

I loathed what it symbolized: defeat.

Chapter Twenty
The Confrontation

On an ordinary Saturday morning, Daddy showed up unexpectedly, sat Mommy down on a hard wooden spindle-backed chair, and stood a few feet away so he could look down on her. It was the intimidating body language of a conqueror.

Accusatory bursts exploded from him. He pointed his index finger at her like a gun. His eyes blazed. Hiding in the kitchen, I was witnessing a persecution.

Daddy's initial assault was mostly centered on the measly household budget and how she'd squandered it. This was wrong! He began to yell at her loudly, his voice escalating as if he was using a bullhorn. He called her a spendthrift, a waster, and a good-for-nothing.

She sat stoically in that old uncomfortable chair, her hands folded in her lap, a wife being verbally abused by her boss, her husband staring her down. Mommy internationalized these terrible scenes. She knew Daddy was too angry, too threatening, to challenge him without repercussions.

Daddy also delved into small-time espionage. He engaged neighborhood spies, phony friends, to tell him "things." He must have paid generously to hear the tattles and insinuations about the lawyer's visit.

He'd seen the laundry stand. He asked Mommy about its origin.

She remained silent and rigid.

When he'd asked me the same question a few days earlier, I'd just shrugged my shoulders. He'd imprisoned me in silence, and, at that moment, he hated my silence.

Daddy was on a warpath.

That laundry stand, in my possession, had a "hidden meaning." That's what he said. He was a suspicious and tumultuous man. His voice thundered the key question again: "Where did you get the laundry stand?" he snarled.

Daddy was a totalitarian. He was an autocrat. He acted as if he was going to hit Mommy, slap her beautiful face. He registered uncontrollable rage. I couldn't stand it. This was out-of-control burn, a fiery rampage.

I zoomed into the center of the husband-wife melodrama, screamed at Daddy to stop shouting, to stop mistreating us. "You don't know anything about being a real Daddy," I screeched as if I had the stamina to face him down. "You're a maniac," I added and immediately regretted it.

Nobody talks back to Daddy like that, especially not the dumbbell.

Daddy leaped toward me like the amateur wrestler he'd once been. I thought he was going to pick me up, throw me over his shoulder, and slam me to the floor.

Instead, he shoved me out of the room with a series of hard jolts to my shoulders. He was jostling a skinny teenage girl hard, pushing her toward the stairs as if he couldn't stand the sight of her. When I fell backward, the wooden stairs banged against my back. It hurt. I started to rise again, to stand up for Mommy.

Daddy pushed me back again, this time with more force. My back was sustaining a series of hard blows from an inanimate object, stairs. Daddy didn't hit me. The stairs did. I heard the jolt of hard knocks against my spine. I tried to get a hold on the banister, pick myself up. I was too puny.

One more hard shove from Daddy and I'd have broken bones.

Mommy shrieked: "Stop!"

Her hysterical voice, oozing uncommon fury, impacted Daddy instantly.

He stopped.

Daddy could change from madman to mellow man faster than a wink. He turned on us and stomped out of the old neglected house as if nothing bad had just happened.

Mommy's truth dawned on me again as I lay sprawled and immobile on the stairs. Mommy was genuinely afraid that Daddy was going to beat us up, kill us. That's one reason she'd said "no" to the lawyer man. He'd engaged spies in the neighborhood, counterfeit pals, to tell him "things." The lawyer, a man with brains, was no match for Daddy, a man of brawn and a dangerous zigzag temperament.

Daddy never touched me again.

But the next day, when we were at about to sit down to Sunday dinner, he was still sizzling with fury. His face, freshly shaved, was flushed. His eyes darted around the small room and focused on us, Mommy and me.

He must have unearthed more whisperings. That style of sleek auto in our grungy neighborhood, a car guarded by a uniformed chauffeur, had produced enough tattling to destroy us.

The table had been set. The food was served. We were seated. Mommy was going to ask me to say grace. She never got the chance.

Suddenly, Daddy stood up straight and with great speed and the expertise of a professional illusionist, he yanked the white tablecloth from the table as mysteriously as a stage magician pulls a rabbit out of a hat. It sounded like a high capacity handgun popping rounds of bullets.

Our miniscule dining room was in total shambles. I was unable to move. Mommy's hands shook uncontrollably. The tiny space had been blown to bits. Pieces of shattered dishes, splattered with food stuck to them, were strewn everywhere.

The flowery wallpaper, studded with those ludicrous palm fronds, was smeared with splotches of moist chicken. Clumps of hot mashed potatoes stained the threadbare Persian rug. Helter-skelter blemishes of splattered gravy stuck to the room's one window and slowly dripped, dripped from the half-drawn shade to the panes to the windowsill.

Mommy should not have asked for, or accepted, the stupid laundry stand.

It was a minor request, ridiculous and extemporaneous. It was meant to stave off a major marriage proposal. Daddy assumed unfaithfulness. It was the opposite. Mommy had been loyal. But her allegiance stemmed from fear of insane repercussions like this.

The wooden laundry stand, the bone of contention, was in my possession. I hung the laundry on the wooden laundry stand. I was the dumbbell responsible for the massive cleanup.

Daddy had stormed off after destroying the dining room and us. But not before pointing his formidable finger, the gun finger, at me.

You're going to pay for his," he grunted.

Chapter Twenty-One
Blood

A bewildering gush of blood was trickling down the inside of my left thigh. I was baffled. I had no idea where it began or what activated it. All I knew is that this blood, whatever its source, had total dominion over me. I was an ignoramus. I didn't know what to do. Instead of urinating, I was peeing blood without peeing.

I was out of control.

The blood, it came in a steady stream, was disgusting, revolting, and humiliating. My sense of decency dissipated. Mommy never spoke to me of coping with an erupting bloodstream flowing from a forbidden place. It was an era when a young girl like me, stuck in isolation, knew nothing about becoming a woman when you least expected it.

I couldn't control the flow. That was horrifying. I couldn't hold it in. I tried. I was frantic. I ran to the bathroom to clean myself up. When I thought I was clean, the blood tumbled out again. I tried to contain the stream with a washcloth held in place. It turned crimson. I was hemorrhaging.

Cold water helps remove bloodstains. I knew that. Hot water makes stains more permanent. Yet, knowing better, I used hot water to scrub my drenched panties, once white and now red. It was a stupid thing to do. I'd panicked. The stains stayed. I wore those soiled panties until they wore out.

When the red stream kept on coming from somewhere inside me, I balled a big bunch of tissues, put it in place, and held my legs together tightly.

It didn't take long for the tissues to turn into drippy red shreds.

I didn't know what to do.

I was bleeding to death.

Hallelujah, I was going to die!

Death! I succumbed happily to the word death, welcomed it. Death would be a permanent release. It was a portent that my miserable existence was coming to an end. Death would mean no more coping with a crazed Daddy. It was what I'd been wishing for: irreversible escape, a permanent disappearance. If I were dead, Mommy would be free of me. She could start over. Maybe the lawyer man would find her again. There would be no kidnapping perils. There would be no suicide schemes. I would rise into the outer universe, become an entity, join my 1,000 angels and follow them.

My bed! I wanted to die in my bed!

I put a raggedy bath towel under me to absorb any leak. Quickly, more quickly than I guessed, the towel was splotched red. The flow was heavy and steady. I jumped off my bed quickly. If I turned the sheets or the mattress red, or if my clothes reddened, I'd die of some kind of in-house punishment more hideous than bleeding away.

Ultimately, this bleeding was a good thing. Mommy had stayed married to save me from being kidnapped. Her sacrifice was enormous. I knew that wasn't the whole story. She was getting more malicious, more critical, toward me now. A gorge too big to straddle was widening between us. There must be much more to Mommy's anger issue than kidnapping.

And I was bleeding to death! Hallelujah!

All I knew about bleeding came from the movies. If a character bled, the plot led to a cemetery rest-in-peace scene. If I died, maybe my 1,000 angels were helping me to die without burning my insides. Maybe I didn't need to drink iodine or gobble that awful nail biter poison that cracked my lips and stung my tongue. Maybe if the bleeding didn't stop, the blood-bath death would be an easy exit.

I wanted one last look at Mommy.

I wanted to say goodbye. This would be a forever goodbye. I loved her far more than she knew. I understood her millstone marriage. I went to her shuddering with fear of the great unknown before me. I trembled. I was bleeding out and trying to say farewell simultaneously.

She was in the kitchen, hovering over the stove, stirring vegetable soup in a big pot. She didn't stop to acknowledge me. Mommy's quick side-glance was glacial. She was like a human ice sculpture, a pretty one. She saw me leaking blood. It dropped out of me onto the linoleum like heavy drops of red rain. It made a puddle.

She said nothing. She continued stirring the soup.

I spoke my truth. I told her I was going to die. I wanted to say goodbye and tell her how much I loved her and how sorry I was to have been born when she didn't want me.

This sorry statement surprised her.

She gazed at me briefly, a question on her lips, but she fell back into the world of chilly silence, our norm. I filled in the blanks.

I apologized several times for all the heartache I'd caused her. Sorry—sorry—sorry! This time I said sorry loud enough for her to hear. I told her she was lovely, and, deep in my heart, I had hoped to grow up and be just like her, the way I first knew her.

In flash thoughts, I remembered when Mommy took me

to kindergarten, and I wouldn't leave her side. I was sure I'd be kidnapped if I were left alone.

"That's all right," she soothed when the teacher tried to coax me with paper doll cutouts. That worked when Mommy was there. When Mommy tried to leave the room, I got hysterical. I was sure kindergarten was a kidnap plot.

"We'll go home and be together, just the two of us," she'd said kindly, taking my tiny hand in hers. I still remember the immense feeling of love I felt for Mommy for not deserting her overwrought crybaby.

In another flashback, I remembered when we walked together, on a spring day, and came across a May Party. Children, moving in a two-by-two sidewalk parade, were chanting "May Party, May Party, Rah-Rah-Rah." I asked Mommy if I could march in the parade dressed like the parade leaders, the king and queen, who wore pastel crepe paper capes and gold cardboard crowns.

The teacher stopped the parade.

She listened to Mommy.

The next thing I knew I was alone, at the end of the parade with no partner, no crepe paper anything. Dejected, I ran back to where Mommy stood waiting and watching. She hugged me and told me never mind, there'd be other May parties. Let's get an ice cream cone. Vanilla.

I loved Mommy the way she had loved me then, unconditionally. She still loved me, but now it was under great duress. She paid a big price for not deserting me. That's why she was always simmering with anger. She was, still torn by her "duty" to Daddy and the lawyer's tempting proposal. She had second thoughts about her second chance.

Daddy changed her totally, made her into a different kind of Mommy.

Now I stood before her and dribbled blood, thinking this was my demise. If I was losing blood and dying, I uttered what I thought were my last words. I told her I'd forgiven her taking Teddy away from me. Goodbye Mommy, goodbye.

The histrionic conversation was one-sided.

Mommy didn't say goodbye. She didn't refer to or define the word menstruation. There was no reference to my becoming a woman. She'd never used the word sex, or how women became impregnated. These subjects were taboo. I'd never asked where babies came from, and Mommy didn't offer any information.

What I gleaned from the movies didn't exist in real life. That's how Mommy dismissed my infrequent signs of sexual curiosity. "It's all make-believe," is the vague way she dismissed me.

She kept me uninformed, unenlightened. Daddy preferred total naiveté. An ignorant girl was more valuable to him than an informed one. The word, virgin, was never mentioned. It was not in my vocabulary. No word regarding my sex was ever voiced or explained.

Mommy's earliest mandate was that I never take off my panties. Never. When I had my tonsils out, the nurses wanted to know why I, a first grader, wouldn't let them take off my panties. When I awoke from the surgery, a nurse asked if I'd like some ice cream. I told her I wanted my panties back.

Daddy thought a young bride would learn it all, in one fell swoop, on her wedding night. That was in my future. I did not know that Daddy picked the groom, and love had nothing to do with it. I did not connect my bloody mess, what was happening to me now, with a wedding. I didn't know that this revolting plasma drip, drip, dripping out of me, gory as it was, represented the onslaught of a new me, a new She, a new woman.

In quick succession, with no eye contact, Mommy issued curt orders.

Go to her dresser. Open the bottom drawer, right side. Get a Kotex from her box. Pin the napkin to a fresh pair of panties.

Kotex? What is Kotex? Napkin? Pins? Panties? How?

"Get two safety pins from my sewing basket," Mommy

added impatiently, continuing to stir the soup.

Kotex was foreign to me. What was its purpose? Kotex turned out to be a sizable "napkin" designed to absorb blood pouring out of a girl? Kotex was a strange object with an even stranger name. How was it worn? How could it stay in place? What happened if there was more blood than Kotex and my clothes became stained for all to see?

Mommy banned Tampons. I didn't know what Tampons were or how they were inserted or where. I looked puzzled. Mommy got impatient. "Don't ever use a Tampon," Mommy cautioned. "You'll lose your virginity."

I didn't know what she was talking about. What was virginity?

When I started to ask questions, she went totally mum. The soup pot was her focus, not me.

I, a total know-nothing, wasn't going to die. I was just a bloody mess.

Maybe if I'd indulged in the forbidden, tried to establish school friendships secretly, I'd have gleaned from their silly female cafeteria chit-chat something about the coming of the blood. All the girls knew all the secret female things.

After school, as I waited for the bus, I'd watch the clubbiest girls whispering among themselves, sharing secrets, as they waited to be picked up by boys with cars.

I was always on the sidelines, observing.

The most alone I'd ever felt, the most rejected, was Mommy's forbidding me to attend my high school's state championship football game. I was forbidden to be part of a young sports crowd. I, the loneliest girl in the world was, as usual, in mandatory seclusion.

It was as if the stadium, three short blocks away from our dreary dark green-shingled house, was on the other side of the universe. Mommy had a particular disdain for cheerleaders. "Bums who kick up their legs for boys," she huffed about the cheerleaders. I was far too introverted, way too shy, far too cloistered to give cheerleading any thought.

That great football day was the only day of my life that I wanted to get lost in the sports crowd, join the football enthusiasts on the bleachers and watch the game of games. I was confined indoors, at home.

Why had I asked to attend a school football game? Didn't I know there would always be always a penance for what I knew were no-no requests?

The sorrow I felt was laced with envy.

I was allowed to stand at a paned window, the equivalent of a crisscrossed transparent wall, and watch closely, yet from afar, an endless crowd of loud, energetic pedestrians, of all ages, marching joyfully, exuberantly toward the field. The window abutted the sidewalk. If the glass didn't separate me from the masses trooping by, waving triangular school flags, I could have reached out and touched them.

I, the dumbbell was being taught the lesson of isolation by example. I could never be a participant in anything public. I was an outcast, an outsider doomed to a life of isolation. I still feel those old twinges of solitary confinement.

All the girls and women whooshing past my pitiful window perch knew about the blood. They were all bloody, every one of them. I bet they all knew what I didn't know. That day-of-denial is inscribed in my memory as profoundly as the day I lost my doggie.

I found the Kotex. It was big and bulky. It had a tab at either end.

I didn't know how to pin this massive cotton rectangle between my legs. Mommy relented, and, in that old kitchen, she showed me how it was done and, when I tried to get used to this unexplained bulk between my legs, Mommy called me a dumbbell.

She was getting more and more malevolent toward me.

I had questions. I wanted Mommy to tell me important things about the blood. I needed some basic information. Instead, Mommy cut me off. She established terrible rules that had terrible consequences. I could not wash myself for a week when the blood was escaping.

"It's very dangerous to put water there," was Mommy's decree,

Why? I asked. Mommy did not answer.

Instead, she said I could take one Kotex and make it last two days. No, I would not have my own box. I would use hers. She would keep count. This would happen once a month on a regular basis until, she said, I was old.

"Why is this happening?" I asked Mommy naively. She said nothing. She turned her back on me.

I didn't wash for a week. I felt filthy. I reeked.

I found out just how offensive I was when a bunch of boys, a bunch of rowdy classmates whom I didn't know by name, followed me home like a pack of wild wolves, chanting loudly and repeatedly in cadence: "You stink like a rotten fish."

It was an open rebuke. Loud. Male. Denouncing. I was overcome with a sense of banishment. I was horrified that I smelled so bad that I'd been singled out for public ostracism. I was an uninformed girl. I knew nothing about mandatory female coping. I was tormented for my disgraceful ignorance.

All the neighbors who lived on the several streets between the school and the dark green-shingled house on the corner, the place of my internment, heard directly from the clump of schoolboys following me that I smelled bad. The news, broadcast loudly by a bunch of boys whose voices had recently dropped an octave, was burn itself. I needed no scarlet letter. Besides, the back of my dress was stained red.

This public shaming continued for days. The boys dispersed only when I reached my corner. I had become a common public spectacle.

I walked straight, head held high, a female stoic who smelled rotten. I thought of myself as burned at the stake, like Jeanne d'Arc. I wanted to run, to get past the public rebuke. I walked ahead of my accusers. They stayed together. They kept their distance. Boys don't want to smell a funky girl close up. Intricate knots of disgrace choked me.

The boy chorus was right.

I stank. I could smell my own stink. I fell into my natural habitat: silence. The whys and wherefores of smelling bad was a personal disaster that I could not, must not, articulate to anybody.

I didn't have to say anything. One sniff of me said it all.

The school nurse noticed those obvious bloodstains, new and old, on the back of my dress.

"Bleeding," I confessed to the nurse. "I'm bleeding."

She was the nurse who healed my burn from the hot iron. She knew I could speak intelligently, but I didn't dare talk much about this lonely dilemma. She empathized with my lack of basic knowledge, my total ignorance, about what was happening to me.

She beckoned me to her office.

The nurse spoke to me gently, explained the meaning of the blood in a simple way that I could understand. She told me I was not alone, that this was every girl's natural function. It had a purpose. It was nothing to cause shame. It just had to be dealt with differently.

I merely nodded. I was greatly relieved to learn that bloody days were on every girl's calendar.

I was shown me to a nice clean bathroom in the back of her office. She gave me a fresh bar of soap and a disposable washcloth and told me it was perfectly all right to wash myself.

She knew that my Kotex should have been disposed of much earlier, that I'd worn it too long. "That's not a good idea," she said. "If you keep yourself clean and wear clean napkins, you won't smell."

I was thankful she didn't use the word stink. I was glad she put free Kotex at my disposal. She gave me a leaflet explaining a girl "Coming of Age." It spelled out the basics of what every young girl needed to know. The blood even had a name. Menstruation.

That's how I found out what being a "She" really meant.

I made a big decision, the first show of defiance I'd ever made in my young life.

I made my own rules. I told Mommy nothing.

I washed every day of my period Nothing bad happened. There was no danger. I used more Kotex than allowed. I also used the free supplemental Kotex from the nurse. Mommy wouldn't put my "filthy panties," as she put it, in the washing machine. I had to soak them in cold water and scrub them by hand myself in the bathroom sink when no one was at home.

Mommy called them my "shame" pants.

I didn't care. I kept myself clean. I had no regrets. This was the first time in my life that I looked after myself. I was disobedient, rebellious, and I didn't feel guilty.

Now Mommy was so brainwashed that she believed whatever Daddy told her. He had been lecturing her lately on the education of women that he described as "a very bad thing with a very bad outcome."

Daddy was a convincing liar. He told Mommy that the more information I had, the more I knew, the more I studied, the more books I read meant that, eventually, I would "look down" upon them, consider my parents to be my inferiors. He told Mommy she would no longer be "my boss," that I'd be hers, and wouldn't that be too bad?

"You want the dumbbell telling you what to do?" he asked. The house was small. I was confined, always lurking in the shadows listening. "The dumbbell will be condescending to us," he pressured.

Mommy believed him. She had been frightened into believing him. She became his cohort. Daddy could not have stopped me so completely, so unmercifully, without Mommy's cooperation. She'd been a competent thinker and an independent woman. Now she was in the process of being destroyed psychologically. His coerciveness had altered her attitude about everything.

People who are destroyed become destroyers. She was swept into the business of destroying the dumbbell. They, Mommy and Daddy, became a brigade of two.

Many years later, when I was a successful young adult, I asked Mommy why she hadn't spoken to me frankly about what menstruating meant.

Her answer was disappointing and surprising. She avoided the word, menstruating altogether.

"It's better not to have sex," she said, regret etched in her voice.

I had not asked that question. I played along.

"Why?" I asked.

"Because you get used to feeling good," she replied.

Satisfying sex trapped Mommy. She was complex woman. She'd been duped into accepting Daddy's stringent rules, the ones that kept her fettered in mind and body. She was tricked into believing our lifestyle was normal or, as once blurted, "natural." But she enjoyed sex. It became entwined in her bondage.

I vowed never to be like Mommy, a trapped wife.

Chapter Twenty-Two
Orphan Boy

I had no clue of future penalties and penances, until Nicholas suddenly became my adopted brother by accident.

He was two years older than me, the only son of one of Daddy's many cousins. Nicholas's parents were both killed instantly in a hit and run car wreck. Overnight he was an orphan. Daddy quickly stepped in. This was his golden opportunity to acquire the son he'd always wanted. Daddy's old politico Mr. Murphy, the Irish ditties man, pushed the adoption papers through the courts speedily and efficiently.

Nicholas came to live with us.

I had always wanted a brother who'd lessen my struggles, pick up his fallen sibling, and champion her. When I washed, ironed, and folded the frequent dirty laundry Nicholas lugged home from college, his comment was pointed: "Dumbbell, you're good at this." He was Daddy's son, not my prized brother.

Daddy had already trained him to treat me as his

inferior, a girl who deserved taunting.

I was to be addressed as the "dumbbell."

The name alone intrigued Nicholas. "That's not fair," Nicholas jabbered once, only once, and my heart jumped for joy.

Daddy laughed at him derisively.

The last thing Nicholas wanted was a disagreement with his newly acquired Daddy. "Always call her dumbbell," Daddy demanded so resolutely that Nicholas, bent on pleasing his new father, readily acquiesced.

Nicholas, Daddy's clone in looks and deeds, was easily converted into a headstrong chauvinist. Nicholas deified Daddy. In turn, Nicholas's needs, desires, and demands were prioritized. No humps and bumps for Nicholas. Daddy was always smoothing his path, making everything easy for him – especially college costs.

I subdued a raging bitterness I'd kept under wraps too long. I envied Nicholas's air of superiority, how he wore a mantle of supreme invincibility and made it seem natural. By comparison, I was pathetic. Nicholas had everything I wanted. I was jealous.

I resented his opportunities.

I coveted his social life, no questions asked about his whereabouts.

Most of all, I begrudged his unbounded freedom that had no time limits. He had the kind of freedom I would never have. He was Tarzan. I was Jane.

Jealousy is its own engine. Defiance, pinched by animosity, made me more aggressive. I wanted to show somebody, anybody, that I was intellectually equal to my new brother.

Staring at a pile of Nicholas's books and his assignment papers, I got a peek at his college world. I craved that world. A loser needs to know what it's like to win. Nicholas was a winner. I wanted to be a winner.

A prank notion hit me. It galvanized my jealousy.

Could I, the girl called "dumbbell," read a book

assignment and write a 2,000-word essay in a few hours? Could I, a she, handle a vital Ivy League college paper as well as a he, and without benefit of political science classes and related lectures? Could I do Nicholas's work on my own, without any instruction, any ancillary information, anything at all?

I have no idea why I thought I could pull off this hoax,

It was early evening, in autumn, a Saturday night. I was alone.

Mommy was sound asleep. Daddy wasn't home.

I scrutinized Nicholas's assignment and noted the impending deadline. It was immediate, the following Monday. I picked up the book designated for the essay, thumbed through it.

As I was considering writing his paper, he was celebrating life at a regional fraternity party at MIT. Fraternities were social passports to lots of rich college girls, and a chance to make abiding friendships with men that sometimes lasted for life.

He was there, partying. I was stuck in the gloomy green-shingled house instigating a mutiny party of my own.

I devoured the book that required the essay.

I pretended, then convinced, myself that his book was mine. I wrote the essay longhand, with the words executed in perfect penmanship. I did not sign it. It was an important college dissertation that I had no moral right to write.

I stuck the finished essay in his book.

The weekend disappeared.

The books disappeared.

When he was back on campus, the facts hit him. He'd forgotten the assignment. He could not meet the looming deadline. He must have opened the book and, shocked, found the finished essay. He could have edited it. Changed things. Added things. He hesitated briefly. He handed it in. He made it his own.

The result was thrilling. He got an "A."

I hoped he'd proffer what I'd written officially as his

own. He was in a prestigious college with a rigorous academic curriculum. I wanted to prove that I could get top grades without half trying. I didn't know I'd ambushed myself, fallen into my own trap.

He telephoned Daddy, told him all the details of my mischief.

Daddy did not chide Nicholas for socializing when his paper was due. No. He told his new son that my punishment would begin as a minor virus and turn into an epidemic.

Nicholas liked Daddy's prophecy.

Malice, and all the innate wickedness it embodies, is more contagious than the flu. I've always been amazed at how speedily hate travels and burns, how combustible it is, how it can incinerate everything in its path.

Not long after he got an "A" for my essay, Nicholas strolled into my room. He walked nonchalantly toward my bureau, grabbed my only treasure—a small Palm Sunday crown of thorns, about three inches in diameter, —and ripped it apart.

I watched, thunderstruck, as he tossed the scraps of my precious possession on the floor, as if it was useless litter.

It was a miniature work of handcrafted art created with meticulous care by my piano teacher, Sister Rosa. She'd woven it the same way she ran her classical music studio in a nearby Catholic convent: with disciplined and painstaking precision.

When she'd given me that beautiful gift, she knew I was emotionally distraught. I was depressed, introspective, and very, very shy. I spoke little. I played the piano well, especially Mozart and Chopin.

Sister hugged me when she gave me that palm crown.

She said it symbolized resurrection.

"How?" I asked, surprised. "How does a girl like me resurrect herself? How does she rise from feeling dead?"

Sister winced. She never pegged me as a girl wanting to die.

"Everything will work out if you allow yourself to be

your own kind of person," Sister said benignly "You have musical talent."

Sister never charged for my lessons. I'm glad I didn't know Daddy had donated a small fortune in her name to the French Church adjacent to the convent. I had loved Sister for loving me without strings.

There were strings. There are always strings. Strings burn.

I'm also glad I didn't know that Nicholas had promised Mommy soon, very soon, after he moved to Washington D.C. to launch his political career, first interning for a southern Senator, that he'd buy her a new house.

I'm glad I didn't know that Daddy had plans to exclude Nicholas from any money obligation regarding any family real estate.

All I knew then was that my Palm crown was gone.

"Martyr!" Nicholas jabbed at me slyly, then again louder: "The dumbbell is a martyr!"

Mommy swooped in to stop the noise.

"*She* called me a bad name," Nicholas fabricated.

He lengthened the word bad into "*baaad.*"

Mommy believed him. "This is all your fault," she poked haughtily to me. I howled and yelped and roared with indignation without making a sound. Cramps crawled into my stomach, burning it. Martyrs suffer. I was a martyr. I was burning.

"Join the Army, dumbbell!" Mommy jabbed the suggestion at me venomously. She didn't want me around the house I'd kept clean. She hadn't wanted me when I was born. She didn't want me now.

Mommy's adopted son, a grown-up substitute for a natural-born son, had assets. It allowed her to avoid the discomforts of pregnancy and the agonizing pangs of birthing. And she'd avoided nine months of ruminating over whether or not she was carrying a boy.

Nicholas took Mommy's arm and the two walked off together contentedly, as if nothing important had just happened.

I picked up the bits and pieces of the crown, stuffed them into a small plastic bag that I stuck in a bureau drawer. Sister Rose's gift had died at Nicholas's hand.

I pitied myself. I was a martyr.

Martyrs are always subject to burn.

Chapter Twenty-Three
Romeo

Daddy's public personae oozed the gentlemanly sophistication that had attracted Mommy in the first place. He was a talented gourmet and sommelier whose cosmopolitan menus were prized. Extravagant spenders, who valued short-term glories, respected his sophisticated talents.

Restaurants he created were run with the sophisticated ease of a cosmopolite. He had flawless manners on the job. When chatting pleasantly with customers, his x-ray eyes picked up on bartenders who thieved or a waitress who showed signs of doubling as a call girl. He was known to fire rambling staff as soon as the work night ended.

That's how he acquired the reputation of restaurateur par excellence. Daddy cultivated the gleaming street angel part of his image with unrelenting vigilance.

What his mass of admirers didn't know is that he had a regular habit of bringing home delicatessen-size baloneys that Mommy sliced awkwardly, by hand, with a big kitchen knife, for thick daily sandwiches. It took weeks to see the end of those Baloneys.

Mommy asked for a small supply of restaurant butter. What Daddy brought home was nearly rancid. When I complained the butter tasted funny, Mommy scolded me. She accused me of being "picky and wasteful," which I was. I couldn't eat those sandwiches. I trashed them when no one was looking.

"See," I heard Daddy brag to Mommy about the Baloney and butter supplies, "I told you I'd be a good provider. "

Daddy liked two kinds of capers. Brined capers, the jarred kind found on supermarket shelves, and capers with glamorous women outside the marriage.

Daddy discovered Mommy, very beautiful, barely nineteen, on a cruise ship sailing towards Mediterranean ports. She was traveling with her parents. He was alone, a bachelor twice her age. He'd seduced her with brash, exuberant promises of wealth that, ultimately, he would lavish on his business, not on her and, certainly, not on me.

Daddy was an intriguer. He wrote love poetry to Mommy after giving her the only valuable that he had onboard, that solid gold Montblanc pen. He closed it in her hand, which he held with both of his, and breathed a guttural growl of sexual desire in her ear. She was a young gullible who was enthralled at being sought-after.

Mommy was not the first, or last, woman Daddy would beguile.

I made this discovery on my own, by chance, when I glimpsed Daddy's private life early one Saturday morning when I was visiting the newest of Daddy's restaurants. I was there, at his insistence, to learn the art of food preparation from a favored sous chef. During a break, I dashed to the Ladies Room, swung open the door, and happened upon a live Titian painting.

A nude woman, a model, and showgirl who'd

waitressed weekends, was assessing her totally naked self in a full-length mirror. It was an erotic scene, carnal. Like all women who used their beauty as a financial passport, she turned this way and that, admiring the mirror reflection of her womanly glories.

If she heard or saw me, or any indication of me in the mirror, she blotted me out. Her breasts were like twin balloons that sprouted erect pink nipples shaped like the rubbery kind on a baby's milk bottle. Her midriff was long and melted into long legs. I had never seen the curve of a woman's bare derriere, which I faced. Her flaming red hair, a sleek pageboy that brushed her shoulders, didn't match her black pubic hair, Curiosity rattled me. I didn't know how such strange hair contradictions happened, or where, or how.

I was also ashamed, sorry—sorry—sorry, that I could not take my eyes off neither the mirror reflection nor the nude herself.

I did not accomplish what I'd come to accomplish. I finally rushed out of the door full of questions about a woman's body. Did Mommy look like that? Would I look like that someday?

I pondered what I'd seen while working in the kitchen, peeling potatoes.

Daddy had private living quarters on the top floor of his business establishment. He stayed there days on end with no explanation except a busy business. Perhaps the amazing nude I saw, the one who pretended I wasn't staring at her, was one of Daddy's illicit romances. Perhaps Daddy had his very own Romeo headquarters.

The sex act remained a mysterious riddle to me. No one, especially Mommy, explained man-woman realities to me. I was kept as ignorant as possible. That was part of my dumbbell legacy. Matinee movies, our occasional escapes, Mommy's and mine, hinted at sexual exploits without the specifics.

I was allowed to talk at home now, but never in Daddy's presence. I wasn't allowed outside the house except with Mommy. Occasionally, she gave me hints about sex – hints I never understood because they were vague pieces of an incomplete puzzle.

I had begged Mommy for a bicycle, a second-hand one. Daddy said no.

"Why?" I asked.

She spoke of his objection as if it was sacred. "Daddy wants you to know that it's unhealthy for a girl to feel the rub of a bicycle saddle between her legs," she said.

"Why?" I asked guilelessly.

Sex wasn't explained fully in the nurse's pamphlet. Only menstruation.

Mommy's eyes were rapt with an excitement I didn't recognize. "Because," she sputtered, "a girl gets used to being touched down there."

I had no idea what she was talking about or how touching and sex were linked. I didn't know what sex was. I never got a bike. I never even learned to ride a bike. I begged Mommy for ice skates. She managed to get me a pair for Christmas. Daddy prohibited my using them. "They're only to look at," he decreed.

"Why?" I asked Mommy before Daddy allocated them, still boxed, on a high shelf in the lowest part of the basement. She didn't answer. Daddy had put the box out of reach, even when I tried on tiptoe. My unattainable skates stayed unused, in their original box, until Daddy, the hypocritical philanthropist, gave them to an orphanage.

"Why?" I asked again before my skates disappeared. I didn't know Daddy was home or that he heard me. He stomped into the kitchen and snarled: "Dumbbells like you can turn into showgirls on ice. Showgirls are bad girls." I knew I was bad, born bad, but I still wanted books, a bicycle, and skates. Everything I wanted, normal things, was a no-no.

Daddy didn't know that I wanted to work with words, not in the entertainment world. I had never been to a live theater or to a professional rink. I didn't know why Daddy turned everything, even the most wholesome things, into a sexual lingo.

I was conflicted about the nude waitress. Should I or should I not be a tattletale? I decided that Mommy should know.

"Men are born hunters," Mommy said when I told her quickly, toning it all down to a sentence or two. "Remember that." She already knew that Daddy was an adulterer. Her almond eyes became vacuous. I hadn't noticed the emptiness before. She must still be thinking regretfully of the lawyer man.

I tried to hug Mommy, but she shied away, rebuffed me.

Daddy didn't know that I planned to make up his unfaithfulness to her, make her believe that, in the end, I wasn't a dumbbell. Someday I would look after Mommy. This was a wish, not a plan. I was not in a position to make plans.

What confused me, what muddled my thoughts of saving Mommy, was that there were times when Daddy became important to her in their bedroom.

The old house, small and raggedy, had thin walls. I did not always hear war there. Sometimes I heard their bed squeak. I heard Daddy's low growls of satisfaction and Mommy's quieter squeals of satisfaction.

Daddy kept me from books, sports, friends. I had no hope of escape. He didn't have a clue that while I was stuck in subservient silence, his dumbbell was observing everything without being observed.

I was getting smarter, more aware of Daddy's formidable leverage. I was desperate to discover why he continued to threaten Mommy.

Chapter Twenty-Four
Friendship

Her name was Lucille.

Dear, dear, Lucille burst like unexpected fireworks into my minuscule orbit and turned my world upside down and inside out.

Mommy and I were strolling toward the shops in town when a middle-aged woman, an acquaintance of Mommy's who happened to be going our way, stopped and chatted about the weather and upcoming drastic sales in the local department store.

I stood in Mommy's shadow, listening. Small talk does not always stay small.

Without hesitation, and with sincere enthusiasm, Lucille asked Mommy, point blank, no preliminaries, if she could take me, by subway, into the city, to a free classical summer concert one evening next week.

Outcasts like me are rarely acknowledged. My heart throbbed. My ears pounded. Lucille's extemporaneous invitation, the first of its kind extended to me, leaped across my heart. This was my first social invitation ever.

The simple joy of being asked, just that alone, stuck to me and remained stuck, the nicest memory of my bullied girlhood.

I'd read about the place Lucille referenced in the many newspapers Daddy discarded. I knew I'd be outdoors, in the city, under the twinkling stars, the skyline bathed in moonlight. A symphony orchestra would be playing beautiful classical music filling the atmosphere, and me, with absolute delight.

The stage sat high, next to a shimmering city river dotted with white sailboats. The sprawling city skyline, a zigzag of gray concrete, was bathed in moonlight. An evening spent in this environment seemed beyond my reach.

Lucille gave Mommy the date-time-place facts. I went a little crazy. But I didn't move. By now, I'd become an expert at hiding myself within myself.

Oh, I craved this miracle. I was starved, ravenous, for a glimpse of life beyond the crowded neighborhood diagonally across Cohen's Market, which sold fishcakes lined up for sale on leaky old newspapers. Even when the windows of my bedroom were closed, I smelled the ever-present waft of fried fishcakes with black ink sauce.

I wanted to breathe clean air. I coveted the blissful sounds of orchestral music created in centuries past. My desire to witness a musical phenomenon out in the open, in the middle of the city, cut deeply. So did a related desire to enjoy amiable sociability. I'd never had the pleasant company of someone who cared about things I cared about.

Just the generous invitation alone, issued so sincerely, made me realize again, with more subdued fury than ever, that I'd been forced to quash my profound needs to observe, and participate in anything creative that sprung from either intuition or the soul.

I'd been cuffed to silence way too long. "No!" was the burn word that ruled my life.

I was sure Mommy would refuse. I wanted to implore Mommy to let me go to the concert with Lucille. I knew if I said a word, if I showed even a smidgeon of longing, the answer would be some version of "No!"

I stood quietly, straight as a beanpole, and made sure my expression was blank and unreadable. I braced myself. Mommy did not sanction jaunts into unknown places. She was the master of clever turndowns. Daddy taught her a million ways to say "No." I knew every one of them.

Yes? Mommy said yes! I thought I was dreaming.

A strain of unfamiliar bliss smoldered inside me. I felt the nicest glow from a fire that didn't burn. It was the fire of comfort, ease, and optimism. It was the burn that destroys constraints. It was the burn of amazing grace. It was the lovely burn that lit the stars. My 1,000 angels were always trying to get me to turn things around, to see old things in a new way.

I hated burn. Now I saw that burn could also mean burning with joy.

I still didn't show any outward sign of excitement. Mommy could change her mind on a whim. I stayed as solemn as if I were at a funeral.

Plans were set quickly.

Lucille, this wonderful woman called Lucille, was a tall brunette, very attractive in a black tailored business suit. She told Mommy she was married for a decade to the chief accountant in City Hall, a fine gentleman. They had no children. It would be a pleasure to have me join her at this concert. She had two reserved seats in the front row.

What she wasn't telling Mommy was what mattered most to me.

The most extraordinary thing about Lucille is that she, a stranger, thought of me, a nobody, as a convivial girl. I could not believe the enormity of social acceptance. I'd never thought of myself as acceptable or amiable, much less a likable companion.

Later I talked this over with myself.

Was it more prestigious to be sought out, invited, or more prestigious to be invited because you were deemed good company?

I told myself that Lucille meant both, that this was a dual triumph, that the girl called "dumbbell" did not appear to be a dumbbell. Lucille had offered me the triumph of friendship and true acceptance plus, big plus, an evening of music.

I have never forgotten Lucille, never will.

Chapter Twenty-Six
Chic

Mommy could be very kind on impulse. Maybe she bore regrets that she'd treated me badly on so many occasions. Mommy never apologized for anything to anybody. If she regretted her behavior, she did endearing things.

She bought a deep purple remnant, one dollar, spied on a department store table laden with discarded fabrics tossed helter-skelter. I knew Mommy had to make room for a dollar lost from her sparse household budget. I was grateful. I didn't dare say thank you. She was moody.

Mommy, in her right mind, gave me a feeling of dignity. A fashion designer by nature, she copied, from a library Vogue magazine photo, a basic Dior shift. I had a gorgeous new dress with a matching bow for my long black ponytail.

I was confounded to realize that nice clothes foster confidence, a fact totally unknown to me. My new clothes made me look good. I felt good. I wanted these good feelings, these twinges of self-confidence, to last forever. I wanted them to become a part of me, the real me.

And there we were, Lucille and I, in heaven on earth.

The amazing components of the concert scene were riveting.

Suspense lurked in the loud murmurings of the audience. The pre-show blabbering sounded like many convoys of chirping birds taking flight. I'd never heard huge crowds of people chattering like noisy flocks of birds.

Although the first sounds of music were soft and gentle, I jumped in surprise. I thought the angels tapped my shoulder, wanted me to know they were around. I was sitting in the front row, surrounded by notes, musical ones. I felt cocooned and wonderful.

The orchestra, forty-five men in crisp white tuxedos, sat in a semi-circle on stage, at attention, in precise rows. The backdrop was astonishing. It was a man-made giant-sized weatherproofed white oyster shell edged in glittering pink lights. What inspired an architect to create a stage setting borrowed from an ordinary oyster shell?

I loved to ponder the genesis of unique ideas.

The instruments, some with secret names I didn't know, made mysterious sounds, enchanting ones, especially when they burst into brief solos. How lucky I was to be where I was.

The music had been created originally for privileged elitists, royals, and titled aristocrats who lived in vast European castles eons ago. Now I, a dumbbell caught in constant bully abuse, was a guest of the same thrilling music. How lucky was I, a poor girl, to be at the centerpiece of a miracle that once belonged to the very rich?

The mere idea that the world beyond Daddy offered opportunity for nothing dumbbells like me was uplifting.

I thought my 1,000 angels must have been floating around, swaying and pirouetting on the beguiling notes that swung high and wide into the atmosphere. I was too—too happy to tell Lucille I was too—too happy.

She knew.

That night, the night of Lucille, I discovered that serious music, the first I'd ever heard in a formal way, has its own set of dynamics. I thought of Teddy scampering for a ball. That was one tempo, a viola. I thought of Teddy being whisked away in a fast-moving truck. The violins whooshed. I fell when I ran after the truck stealing Teddy. That was another tempo, a crash of cymbals.

I heard other divine tempos that seemed ethereal.

Chords could be played evenly or broken into single notes.

Sharps and flats could become harmonious.

The glorious sounds that I absorbed like a sponge were metaphors for human passions. I heard joy. I heard tragedy. Each piece seemed like a little vignette borrowed from a storybook. The rousing music swallowed me, dazzled me.

Pulsating drumbeats, the shrillness of metallic trumpets juxtaposed against the lowest notes of a cello, suggested battlefields, war zones, and reddish streams.

I heard the gentle solace of prayer that was not a hymn.

I heard the tapping sounds of exotic dancing of lovely nymphs whirling around a bonfire.

I heard shattering thunderstorms with winds whipping through a vast black forest. I heard shocked trees shaking at the prospect of being uprooted.

I heard the exquisite lull of soothing violin music that invited sleep, those charming lullabies and cradlesongs written to dazzle adults.

How was it possible to hear narratives in music without words?

The music enabled me to see images with my ears and discover how creativity, in whatever form, has remarkable links to every emotion involved in the human journey.

When the bassoons hit low notes and the tubas joined in, I heard the sobbing sounds of human sorrow. I thought this music was talking directly to me.

The orchestra leader, his back turned, was in total

control.

It wasn't like Daddy's forced control. It was inspired control.

Everyone shielded by the walled oyster shell displayed a palpable willingness to blur and blend their individual talents to their leader's bidding.

The maestro was the inspirer, the *steerer*, the commander-in-chief, and the supreme leader of dozens of musicians. He had inherited the inner power of some long-ago god who ruled by genius.

He raised a stick.

It metamorphosed into a magical baton.

His was the secret language of gestures. What the baton didn't say, his hands did. It was a stupefying scene of total togetherness. I'd never been part of a team, any kind of team. I knew nothing about collaboration. Can a loner like me ever become immersed in a focus greater than herself?

How was it possible that one man, perched on a podium, had been blessed with the astounding clout and knowledge and confidence to direct dozens of orchestra players to do his bidding in sync?

This work was not based in rationale.

He was the spiritual master who emboldened his players to do his exact bidding at the exact moment in the exact way he commanded. This was something sacred.

The maestro's level of extreme professional control intrigued me. Control requires discipline. Dedication too. You can't be in control if you don't have self-control. That's where control starts, inside your head. It includes your heart and soul, the places of passion.

I was so glad I'd looked up the word "soul" before Daddy destroyed the dictionary.

Chapter Twenty-Seven
Intuition

Abruptly, for no good reason, the word "control" seriously sidetracked my thoughts. Daddy was the ultimate controller.

Daddy! Oh my god, I caught a glimpse of Daddy.

There he was, a fuzzy image of him, indistinct, on the telephone, yelling at Mommy who was cringing. His subliminal image, that's what it was, lured me back to his obnoxious idea of supremacy. "The dumbbell has to be housebound at all times," he'd told Mommy lately when I'd been close by. That's what he was saying now, on the telephone.

"Go away!" I ordered silently to the phantom image.

Mentally, I elbowed Daddy out of my immediate surroundings. I willed him gone by blocking him out. This was the first time that I realized that the power of the imagination could, if you directed it, become a control mechanism.

My concentration swung back to the concert.

The music lifted me to the stars, a whole world made of stars, and I cavorted among them, hopscotching from one star to the other

Unexpectedly, the music stopped. It was intermission time. I was back with Lucille, sitting next to her, spellbound by what I was witnessing.

I wondered, more seriously than I'd ever wondered, how creative people control their medium, dip into a magic well of creativity and emerge with something utterly beautiful.

How could music be a form of such rapture and escape?

The word, "e*scape!" assaulted me.*

I automatically related "escape," to my forever-wish, to escape from Daddy.

Daddy! Oh my god! There he was again in the same meddling telephone image, an odd repeat of the first specter. Why was a vision of Daddy bullying Mommy and obstructing my joyful evening?

The second interruption came and went speedily.

I thought of my angels.

Maybe the 1,000 angels saw what I saw. Maybe they blocked what was a premonition. Had something bad happened at home? Why was I getting visions of Daddy bullying Mommy exactly the way he bullied me?

I forced myself to return to the great goodness of the music that had just resumed. This was not a night of bad and burns. It was a sweet musical evening that revealed the human condition with glorious sounds. This was another way of being told a story.

I lost myself in the magnificence of it again.

Composers, I started to memorize their names from the program, knew how to harness their most vague impressions. They dared to construct sounds of everlasting beauty that began with a personal notion, an overheard phrase, an unexpected cadence of conversation, a word, a thought, a sight, or an idea.

I wanted to do that kind of work.

I'd like to make music with words and paint images that made music without words. That night, at the concert, I saw a suggestion of a later me, the grown-up me, the woman I wanted to be someday.

Composers not only had their methods of communication, they used punctuation marks just like writers do.

Quick breaks in sections of music required commas, small pauses, like taking a short breath between thoughts in a sentence. The music was full of perfectly placed commas.

I actually heard exclamation points.

They blasted from trumpets brandishing flashes and crashes. After the exclamation points ceased, their sounds hung in the air, the way actual exclamation marks look, surprised.

Composers used periods oddly.

One period at the end of a musical story wasn't always enough.

I heard a magnificent flourish of periods that made you think it was the end when it wasn't. It stopped for a split second and was repeated. The unexpected surprise of two identical endings was a gift.

Only because the beguiling music unbound the ties crippling me, I let my imagination fly.

I was destined to be a creative inventor, a communicator. I felt it in my bones. I was going to pioneer new things, push past boundaries, turn ordinariness into the extraordinary. When? How? What? These questions were scattered among my many unknowns.

When others started to exit, I didn't move. The music continued to ring in my ears. It had chiseled itself into my imagination. I wanted more. But the splendid program was over.

Lucille sensed my regret.

"Would you like some ice cream?" she asked ever so kindly.

Oh, would I!

Chapter Twenty-Eight
Night Magic

We walked across a massive park where Swan Boats paddled people slowly across what looked like a small lagoon where fairies lived. Lucille said she would take me for a ride if Mommy agreed.

"No!" I already heard Mommy's future "No!"

I didn't tell Lucille that luxury outings were almost impossible for dumbbells like me. I looked up at Lucile and smiled with my eyes. My thank you was written there.

Lucille was trying to save me and didn't know it. I thought her name ought to be Grace, as in Amazing Grace. I even thought maybe, maybe, she was one of my 1,000 angels in human form.

The noisy nighttime city had enormous glamour.

Throngs of fashionables strolled under the old-fashioned lamplights. Fancy cars and impatient taxis thrummed their way through the wide city streets. Honking horns sounded vaguely like bass drums of the orchestra.

Nighttime meant bedtime for me. But the city was illuminated by intriguing lights and the shiny full moon. Lucille, dear Lucille, had opened my eyes to worldly scenes and possibilities I didn't know existed,

We strolled to a nearby café lit with flickering make-believe candles. The tables had white linen tablecloths and matching napkins. The waiters, male and female, wore black tuxedos.

Lucille asked me what flavor of ice cream I liked.

Vanilla, please, I said. My heart was twinkling with the joy of marvel. I had no idea that cafes like this existed or that I'd ever frequent one.

The ice cream did not arrive in a cone. It came in a tiny crystal dish sitting on a white paper doily nestled on a little silver tray and a matching spoon.

Elegance!

Next time you wish on a star ask for everything elegant, I thought and smiled at Lucille. She knew she'd made me happy. The excitement and inspiration of the evening made my natural inquisitiveness surface. Question after question poured out.

Lucille told me what she knew about the composers listed on the program. When she thought the seriously researched biographical information was too much for me to absorb instantly, she told me frivolous things.

Mozart had a pet dog when he was nine.

"I had a dog named Teddy," I ventured.

"Did you love him?" Lucille queried. "Oh, yes," I managed.

Vivaldi, she said, was a priest who had red hair, an oddity in Italy where dark hair prevailed. His peers, who looked different, taunted him.

I only nodded.

I wanted to tell Lucille that bullying still exists, that no one ever stamped it out. I wanted to confide in Lucille, tell her that Daddy was a bully. I didn't dare. My 1,000 angels knew all my truths. That was solace enough.

Lucille told me that Johann Sebastian Bach fathered twenty children. I giggled. Would Daddy still call me "She" if I were one of his many, many "she" offspring? Lucille didn't know what I was thinking. But when I giggled, she giggled too.

Franz Joseph Haydn, the teenager, once cut the braid off a fellow musician. It caused a ruckus.

I didn't tell Lucille that when a sixth-grade classmate handed me shearing scissors and asked me to cut her hair, I chopped it to smithereens.

My friend's angry mother dragged her wailing daughter to our front door and hollered about my nerve and, especially, about my obvious lack of hairdressing skill.

"Look!" she bellowed to Mommy, gesturing to her agitated daughter. The girl was running her hands through here-and-there clutches of hair scattered among nearly bald spots.

I expected and deserved the worst. Mommy replied only that she regretted the incident, but hair grows back, doesn't it? When Mommy closed the door she started to laugh. She saw comedy in my naughtiness, in my creativity gone radically wrong. I thought how contagious laughter is, how it a natural medicine, a kind of happy release.

I didn't tell Lucille the whole story, just that I had once cut a classmate's hair, and the results were very, very bad. Lucille and I laughed together.

Lucille seemed to understand my crushed streak of boldness, the part of me that Daddy especially scorned. She told me that I had a sense of adventure. She spoke to me gently like the angels had spoken.

"Girls like you become explorers," she said." They blaze trails that start trends." I knew then that this stranger, Lucille, saw the skeleton of my inner machinery waiting to be charged, to start its journey.

I became serious. Lucille was, for a moment, a stand-in for a Mommy. I had an intense desire to talk, not in reams, just a little frank talk.

"Once I had a dictionary," I said lightly. "I wanted to know the meaning of the word 'soul.' I've always wanted to study where the soul exists."

"Go on," Lucille said approvingly,

"I play the piano, you know, and on a sheet of music I saw the word staccato. I looked that up too." Lucille asked if I remembered what it meant. "Short loud sounds," I replied. Lucille smiled so cordially that I felt a jolt of pride. I was hearing approval, encouragement.

It loosened the tongue that Daddy had muted.

I told her that I thought the musical geniuses, the ones whose music I'd just fallen in love with, were human beings, like us, but that they knew how to escape to other worlds, reach other dimensions known only to them.

Lucille told me that creative people create their own realms.

I wanted to know more, much more about everything, anything. Lucille looked at her watch. It was time to go home.

Sorry—sorry—sorry, I blurted, the humiliating word Daddy made me say over and over, when he felt I should repent for reasons unknown. I said sorry—sorry—sorry as naturally as most people say hello.

"Sorry about what?" Lucille asked quietly. Her tone was tender, caring. "You've got nothing to be sorry for," Lucille responded. "Don't be sorry for things that don't connect to a real apology."

I told Lucille I meant I was sorry, sorry that the evening was ended. "Happiness doesn't come to an end. It becomes a happy memory," she replied. I really wanted to tell her about Daddy and how sorry he made me feel.

I didn't dare.

"We'll do more fun things together again soon," Lucille promised.

Chapter Twenty-Nine
Explosion

A trolley brought us home.

We walked toward the house, chatting happily about the music we'd just heard.

The old-fashioned streetlamps were turned on here too. It didn't seem like my old street where the houses inclined toward each other, and everybody knew everything about everybody. The street seemed more pleasant than usual.

I floated on a euphoric cloud of discovery. The symphonic music gave me one of the happiest moments of my early teens. I had been granted my wish. Not only did I escape, I found myself in the world of magnificent sounds that startled my imagination and brought me, the real me, to life.

As we walked, I thought, Lucille will always be my friend. I had a friend once, Teddy, who was kidnapped. No one is going to kidnap Lucille. The word, kidnap assaulted me.

Kidnap, kidnap, kidnap.

Mommy was waiting on the front porch, sitting in an old wooden rocking chair that vibrated back-and-forth, back-

and-forth much too fast.

Something was wrong.

When she caught sight of us, she skidded down the front stairs so fast I thought she'd fall and immediately, with no warning, launched into a screaming fit of sobering hysteria.

She was loud. She was raucous. She was mad. She hurled a jumble of accusatory words at poor, stupefied Lucille. Mommy was throwing one of her fits, the kind Daddy goaded her into, the kind he heaped on her himself.

Curled somewhere inside Mommy's fiendish rant, I heard her say the word *"kidnap."* Her old fears, the original ones Daddy held over her head like a sword, burst to the forefront. "You could have kidnapped her," Mommy fumed.

She was incoherent, crazy.

This was the first time I wanted to tell Mommy to shut up, to go into the house, drink the magic potion in Daddy's liquor cabinet, and just shut up.

I didn't say what I wanted to say.

Instead, some awful force pushed me down into the awful hole of silence. All I could think of to say was sorry— sorry—sorry. I'd broken away from Daddy's jail for an evening. I'd enjoyed a concert and a civil conversation with a fine woman. I wasn't sorry. I didn't say I was sorry.

I shook inside the way Mommy's hands were shaking now so visibly, so pitifully. My heart wasn't a heart anymore. It perished without the help of iodine or fingernail poison.

"You had no right to snatch my child into the blackness of the night," Mommy blared at Lucille. "Late! Fifteen minutes late! What were you doing in those fifteen minutes?"

Her voice was rife with suspicion.

"You were walking too slowly down the dark street! What was going on? What did you tell her?"

Mommy yowled these idiotic accusations at Lucille without conscience or remorse. It was as if she didn't know, or had forgotten, where I'd been and that she okayed it.

"A girl her age, a young teenager accompanied by a mature woman, has very, very bad implications," Mommy said insultingly. "Shame! There is shame here!"

What did Mommy mean? What shame?

Why was I, or Lucille, supposed to be ashamed? Lucille couldn't have been nicer. I had done nothing wrong. Finally, I heard the sorry—sorry—sorry words inside me tumble out. But I didn't know what I was sorry about. I could not tell Lucille directly how sorry I was that Mommy was making such a deplorable spectacle of herself, and us, hurling such contemptible allegations.

I just kept on saying sorry—sorry—sorry.

Mommy's loudness and the lewdness of her suggestion drowned out everything, even my sorry—sorry—sorry.

Why was Mommy so out of her mind?

There had to be a reason, something had to set her off.

Lucille got the gist of Mommy's madness, the suggestion of lesbianism, and she stood by nobly without flinching. This implication was way, way out of bounds. Lucille was no longer willing to deal with Mommy's unfounded and horribly twisted tirade.

She looked at me with colossal pity and walked away. I'd just been kidnapped from a friendship with Lucille. It had nothing to do with my being kidnapped by Daddy and given away to one of the aunts. But it burned as bad, so bad, that I stumbled in shock.

Mommy grabbed me as if I were a ragdoll, dragged me up the front stairs, All I could think to say as I was being thrust back into jail was my usual sorry—sorry—sorry.

Suddenly the truth dawned.

The angels had tried to forewarn me. Twice. Those two interruptive premonitions that I'd brushed away like specks of unwanted dust were tip-offs.

Daddy must have telephoned the house and Mommy, believing she had done the right thing, a delightful thing, told him that I had gone to a concert with Lucille. All hell broke loose. Daddy was wreaking havoc again, disgracing Mommy's judgment in his usual toxic way. He'd been on one of his rampages. I knew what it sounded like.

"You sent her off into the night with a strange woman who had bad sexual intentions toward her?" Daddy had probably roared into the receiver, directly into Mommy's ear. "Didn't you say 'No?' Did you forget, 'No?' Didn't we agree that 'No!' applied to everything about the dumbbell?"

Daddy had to have his revenge. I'd left his confines. I'd bypassed his jurisdiction.

He destroyed Mommy first, and she, in turn, destroyed me.

Why did Daddy always make an innocent pleasure sound like sex? I never understood that. Daddy had panicked Mommy into believing I could become a lesbian, that Lucille would teach me "tricks" and if I weren't already a sex maniac with the boys, I would be soon.

I didn't know any boys. I didn't know Lucille except as the nice concert lady. I didn't know the sexual practices of lesbians. I didn't know what boys and girls did sexually. I didn't know anything except that I loved the symphony.

Daddy made Mommy promise never to give me a little space, a taste of freedom. "No!" was even the answer when my French teacher picked her four-star students and created "The French Club," one-half hour of reading advanced French, under her jurisdiction, after school, one day a week. "No!" Mommy decreed unreasonably. "You can't tell what can happen in half an hour."

Lucille was the only person who realized that I had no rights.

I had nothing. I was nothing.

"Dumbbell!" my mother had squealed as she yanked me into the house the one and only time I ever saw Lucille. Sorry—sorry—sorry, I said to myself, for myself. I was sorry to be me. I was back where I belonged. I had no right to go to a concert or, in fact, to go anywhere.

Sorry—sorry—sorry.

Chapter Thirty
Quiet

Silence wasn't the black box Daddy thought it was.

Mommy, and certainly not Daddy, had no idea how alert I'd become, how impressionable. What I heard, what I saw, was now stored in the lobe of the brain that imitates an insatiable file cabinet.

When I was engulfed in Daddy's imposed silence, when I complied with his order to shut up permanently, my eyes and ears worked in perfect unity. I could sense people's character, their attitudes, and prejudices, as if they were see-through. I read between the lines of conversation. I grasped what was not being said with far more accuracy than before.

I drifted into wonderful trances. Gossamer voices spoke to me.

I saw sparkling lights where there weren't any. I saw aged wooden doors, embellished with intricate carvings, fly open and invite me in. I saw lush green tropical landscapes pop up out of nowhere. I saw showers of flowers fall out of the sky.

Daddy didn't know that I spoke to myself, heard myself speaking back to me. He didn't know that when he commanded me to shut up, I could shut out the world, his world, and listen to what was going on in my world.

He didn't know I had pleasurable reveries.

He didn't know that I could focus on any drawing in the school dictionary, those postage-size penned illustrations sitting next to a word, and hold the image in a long, unblinking stare. He didn't know that I could anesthetize myself into recalling that image at will. He didn't know I was playing instant recall or, perhaps, cultivating a photographic memory.

Words that I couldn't understand in the school dictionary, the one I hoarded during lunch breaks, I was able to unscramble by sounding out the letters. He didn't know I, the dumbbell, played my own kind of charades before I knew it was a bonafide game.

He didn't know that I valued the tranquility of silence or that it enabled me to hear 1,000 angels speaking to me, only me, in one fragile breath, singly, or in unison, and that I heard them clearly.

He didn't know that the magic cloud of 1,000 angels seemed to leap and fall and tumble out of the atmosphere, hurdle through the dark forest, dangle from the sun or spring from the stars.

He didn't know they navigated oceans without getting wet.

He didn't know they made snowballs out of surf.

He didn't know they snatched stars from the sky and left them under my pillow.

He didn't know they landed out of sight, in the deepest recesses of me, and glued my brokenness with a sugary concoction that smelled of roses.

He didn't know they gave me a sailboat that I commandeered on my own, without lessons, through great heave-ho ocean storms that tested my ability to edge forward no matter what.

He didn't know they prattled invisibly through the house, surrounded me in a circle, making the heaviest of my chores light and fast.

He didn't know how they comforted me with whispers of sugary words that were like no other balm on the real earth.

He didn't know that my 1,000 angels strewed notions of great expectations in my path.

He didn't know they were not the angels of Bible lore.

He didn't know they flew without wings, faster than jet planes, on their own fuel.

He didn't know they moved invisibly, in a flurry of floating togetherness and assured me, over and over, that I was not alone.

He didn't know they always appeared to be delicate but were made of something indestructible like steel that happened to be white.

He didn't know my 1,000 angels could reach me in a way no one else could, that their 1,000 watts were like a magnifying glass that unmuddled my muddles and unjumbled my jumbles.

He didn't know they never called me dumbbell. He didn't know that my 1,000 angels had taken the three letters, *s-h-e*, Daddy's old hex, and tagged on *three more letters, i-l-a*. The angels called me Sheila.

He didn't know that the 1,000 angels, or the one speaking for all of them, reminded me that the word "She," contained the word he. They spoke to me of Eve and Adam, not the other way around. He didn't know they put "She" first and said there would never be a "he" without a She who menstruated.

He didn't know that one night all of them, as one of them, jumped over the moon, whirred past many constellations, and landed on my bedcovers to be sure I was having sweet dreams.

Once, when I was almost asleep, I told my 1,000 angels

that I wished they'd help Mommy who, like me, was a victim. They told me simultaneously, in sublime clarity, they would reach her through me. They knew I loved Mommy even when she was unlovable.

He didn't know that they transported me to other worlds charged by splendid forces I knew nothing about and that they told me that one day I would create a world of my own.

Daddy didn't know that I believed them.

He had other plans.

Chapter Thirty-One
Pearls

Mid-morning, on a warm early spring day, Mommy walked out toward the back yard and instantly collided with Daddy.

He'd left for his office much earlier. He was breathless, hurried. He was carrying a small brown paper bag. Something baffling was going on.

When Mommy and Daddy weren't dueling, when they were temporarily satisfied with each other, a jewelry gift usually came into sharp focus. Mommy had ordered a pearl necklace, real ones.

I never heard the request. I saw it being fulfilled here, her wish come true, from behind the nearby kitchen screen door where I, the silent bystander stood half-hidden, all ears.

Daddy made his presentation hurriedly, impetuously, and crudely.

He simply handed his wife a grocer's small brown paper bag, used.

Our backyard, surrounded by those rickety triple-deckers inclining toward one another could easily be mistaken for a facsimile of a theatrical stage set. Nosey locals were able to enjoy a dramatic husband-wife spectacle being played out before them. Their front windows were the best seats in the house.

Mommy opened the bag. It was stiff. The paper crackled.

She pulled out a string of luminescent pearls, real pearls, lovely pearls, and quickly dropped them back into the bag again. Disappointment danced across her pretty face.

Daddy had chosen the wrong moment, the wrong packaging, the wrong pearls.

"I don't want these pearls," Mommy huffed in righteous indignation. "These pearls are one size pearls," Mommy sulked and raised her protest a little too loudly. "I told you I wanted a necklace of *graduated* pearls."

Her tone was petulant. She even pounded the dirt ground, still hard, with her right high heel. I'd never seen her instigate a Daddy dispute. She acted nervy.

But the "little woman," Daddy's sarcastic reference to Mommy being of little importance, had stopped her despot in his tracks. She appeared not to give a damn. She dared to provoke him in a contentious way. Maybe Mommy knew she was safe from immediate retribution. They were in broad daylight, in an open public space.

Daddy was furious, red-faced, and trapped outdoors, unable to be the house devil in public where he was always the street angel. He knew that this was not the place to execute marital havoc that would cast aspersions on his public image of supreme generosity.

I was a high school senior then, just turned seventeen and, in the '50s, every girl everywhere coveted real pearls. They still do.

I wasn't thinking beyond graduated pearls. I was privy to an inconvenient tiff, that's all. Hey, I thought, there's no tangible reason to panic. This is just a spat.

Yet, I don't know why, I panicked. Bullied people

develop super-sensitive antennae. They sense "something" is brewing even when they don't know what the brew is.

What shook me up was that Mommy had locked glances with me at the precise nanosecond she'd uttered the word "graduated."

A rash thought bumped into my head. I felt sucker punched. The word, "graduated," as in her graduated pearls, was somehow being linked to my being "graduated," as in my high school graduation.

This was a wacky omen, undecipherable. It loomed close. I was fearful.

Lately Mommy took perverse pleasure in testing my ingenuity. She talked in riddles, tried to stump me. Oh, this could be some sort of cryptic riddle… something that presaged a crippling scheme. Oh.

Living with my fiercely dysfunctional parents, I knew that little things could mean a whole lot of bad. Minor innuendos like the unjustified blink of an eye, a half-spoken phrase, a question left dangling, a minor posture shift, the lift of an eyebrow, or , like just now, even the undue emphasis on one particular word, "graduated," could have major ramifications.

I glanced at Daddy.

He was a double-dealer, a schemer. He'd probably gone to the police chief who had access to a padlocked room where unclaimed stolen goods were secured in locked cases until the claims deadline expired.

Unclaimed goods, mostly precious jewels, were then sold cheaply. You had to know the right people to get access to that bolted room.

The cops in charge of confiscated precious jewelry were Daddy's pals.

Daddy had gone to some trouble. He expected a show of public affection from his wife. On the other hand, Mommy reveled in the showdown she'd created. She liked the neighbors to think she now had the upper hand, that she could handle the "Big Boss" in any showdown.

She had turned into another kind of Mommy after the lawyer's sentimental proposal. She was bitter. She became more revengeful and savvier. Cunning hung in the air and misted it with distrust. Mommy played the matriarch now. She practiced Mommy power. She exerted Wife Power. Hardness set her lovely rosebud lips in a straight hard line. Her brown eyes, lashed long, glowered instead of glittered.

She was still so beautiful. I tried to ignore the changes in her personality. But Mommy flouted her new self. She'd become steely.

"Our *deal* is off," Mommy pouted while shoving the brown paper bag back into Daddy's hands. I was drowning in misgivings. She turned her back on Daddy, walked the few steps to the back door, brushed past me, and disappeared.

When Mommy flung the word *"deal,"* at Daddy, she made direct eye contact with me again. Her eyes flashed a warning signal. Did the words "graduation" and "deal" contain an encrypted message? Was there a mysterious scheme brewing?

I existed in a more guileful environment now. Too many times I'd heard Daddy assuring Mommy: "Someday we'll be able to use her." Instinctively I knew that the words "deal" and "graduated" centered on me.

Together they'd hatched a treacherous plan to stop me in my tracks.

I don't know how I knew it. I just knew.

I wondered if the angels knew.

Chapter Thirty-Two
The Dismissal

The next morning, before I left for school, Mommy was wearing a necklace of graduated pearls with her pink wrap-and-tie bathrobe, drinking English Breakfast Tea, lost in thought.

My reaction to the graduated pearls was denial.

Linking Mommy's "graduated" pearls to my being "graduated" was unfounded. I'd made it up. Silly girl! My dread had no basis. Mommy's new pearls were lovely.

Yet my intuition was in full swing. It told me that I was lying to myself. Something was going on behind my back. Fear jabbed at me. I couldn't control it because I didn't know the cause.

Emotionally abused children have special radar. It presages back stabbings, unforeseen and unexpected. It rattles loud, disturbing signals familiar to a bullied girl. The amplified sound waves on my radar were blasting away.

I'd been warned.

I was on the verge of being blindsided, that Mommy and Daddy were in cahoots, and that I was going to end up being trampled by a herd of stampeding horses. I must have done something bad. Therefore, something bad was going to happen to me.

Still, I said cheerily, "Bye, Mommy! I'm off to school." No answer. Bad!

When the bus rolled, I suspected that it was moving me toward an unknown penalty. I was on the brink of being seriously sidetracked.

When I wobbled into the school building head down, I teetered through the halls toward my homeroom class. I was so discombobulated that I couldn't walk straight.

My homeroom teacher spied me swaying toward the open door.

She jumped from the platform on which her desk sat, swerved toward the door, which she almost slammed, and further barred my entry by blocking the threshold.

This was mighty body language, the equivalent to a "no entry" traffic sign.

That teacher, known for her sternness, looked more dour than usual. Icicles dripped from her voice when she ordered: "Go to the dean's office immediately." She didn't move until I turned my back and walked toward my destiny. I heard the homeroom door open and close from a distance

I was cool, a fake cool, when I entered the Dean's office. I knew that my graduation and Mommy's graduated pearls were somehow connected and that the awful details were about to be revealed.

The Dean motioned to a chair opposite her desk.

When I sat down, she praised me so passively that I knew her compliments were a prelude to some kind of execution. "You've scored among the top ten of the school's recent IQ testing," she said dispassionately." I've informed your father of your very high standing."

Daddy! Daddy and the Dean had been in communication!

I froze as I burned.

"I've also reminded your father that you'd won the senior class medal for spelling," the Dean said casually. She looked down at a pile of papers on her desk, not at me.

Her pause was way too long. The downward spiral had begun.

I'd brought the spelling medal home, proud. Mommy ignored it. I kept it on top of my bureau for days before tossing it in the rubbish. My accomplishments were considered worthless. I was worthless.

I'd applied for college scholarships here, there and everywhere. I'd had no responses. Daddy must have received the reply letters and trashed them. Or maybe he showed them to Mommy and together they'd hatched a plan to destroy me before they'd destroyed the letters I'd never see.

"Your father," the Dean was saying in an unsympathetic gray monotone, "has removed you to a course lower than your four-year college major."

My throat closed. I couldn't breathe.

The Dean, a matronly woman with fluffy white hair, was wearing an all-black dress, funereal, as she delivered the deathblow. She was in charge of a distinguished high school of 2,000 students. This dean had a reputation of treating star students with an adroit finesse. At that moment, she was a hypocrite. She'd abandoned me. She never said she'd tried to convince Daddy I had potential.

I paled a deadly white.

She knew that she had to get this execution over as quickly as possible.

"You've almost completed the College course, and with distinction," she admitted, shuffling those papers on her desk, avoiding my steady stare. "Today, you're going to join The Commercial Course."

Here she cleared her throat. "You'll be taught how to type and file."

Daddy was in the room! Typing and filing was in the

room! Putty was in the room! "Clerking" was in the room! Daddy always said the highest calling of a dumbbell was "clerking." Everything I never wanted was in the room! This was the "deal" he'd made with Mommy!

I tried to console myself. Useless.

Dreamers like me, especially those who've been severely abused emotionally survive by living in another world of their own making. I'd stored my first primal writings and paintings in a locked metal box under my bed. They were the sum total of my modest genesis, raw, the beginning of the real me. I planned to build on them, somehow, when Daddy wasn't looking. A pipe dream.

Defeating thoughts flashed through my subliminal self.

Daddy had just snuffed out my dreams. He didn't care how or where I'd hoarded my first tries at being creative. One telephone call and he'd incapacitated me.

I fell back into the dean's office, paying attention to my execution.

The Dean was issuing the final throes of fulfilling Daddy's orders, thrusting me on a new unwanted trajectory.

"Home economics courses are included," she was saying matter-of-factly.

I was already adept at housekeeping.

"Cooking and sewing classes are also available," the Dean added.

I could prepare a meal. I could mend socks. I could hem anything. I could cut the pattern of a dress with an accuracy that Mommy envied. I helped her with our little budget. I knew all about home economics.

It was true. I was a dumbbell. My future had no future.

This whole encounter was beyond destructive and offensive. It was contemptible. It was as if I'd walked through a glass door and lay crushed under a thousand shards of glass sharper than knives.

Where were my angels now?

The dean stretched over her desk and handed me a neatly typed card. All the class information and room numbers that I needed now, at this melancholy moment, were clearly typed on it.

The Dean didn't want a broken-hearted senior with fine college-preparation grades in her midst. It was too disturbing. She had a conscience. But morality is so easily bought by gifts. Daddy must have sent her a case of fine liquor or given her passes for a string of free candlelight dinners.

The Dean stood up, a gesture of dismissal.

The meeting was finished. So was I.

Stunned, alone, and demeaned at school, I figured out the parental "deal" back home.

Daddy must have bribed Mommy with the pearls. She'd agreed to have me downgraded, and degraded, just before graduation. He must have promised that I'd eventually give her a little salary. Instead of struggling to make ends meet, instead of being loudly labeled a "spendthrift," Mommy would be a bit more comfortable. There was no college in my future. I was going to be forced to take a job, the kind that high school dropouts get.

Damn Daddy!

In the past two weeks, I'd pleaded with Mommy to convince Daddy to let me go to a communications college or a state college that offered art and writing classes. I would take a year off, earn money, pay my own tuition, and pursue a scholarship. I'd do it on my own.

"Ask Daddy yourself," she'd shot back

I asked. I was beyond stupid to ask.

Daddy stood in the kitchen dressed in a business suit. A button had flown off one cuff of his blue button-down shirt. He'd taken off his jacket, stood militarily with palpable indifference to me, close by. Mommy kneeled in dutiful submission, sewing a button on that cuff.

Their togetherness pose was more revealing than ever. Mommy, the seamstress, seemed so obedient, so weak. Daddy, the unchallenged king, was enjoying her slavish attention.

Please, I'd begged, could I speak to you, Daddy?

He didn't answer. I could not look him in the eye. I was a trembling wimp. I was overly deferential and timid and panicky. I looked down at my beat-up penny loafers and white bobby socks, gathering courage. This entreaty was the most important beg of my teenage life. It was my one and only chance to step up, to learn, to *do*.

And I was asking my enemy, the man who hated me for not being born male, to help me get to college or, at least, sanction the idea of college.

My plea was made. I'd rehearsed it. It was direct. No frills. Brief.

When I looked up, when I saw my towering Daddy looking down at me, his face was contorted, buckled into something that was a cross between extreme derision and unconscionable disrespect. His firstborn, his seventeen-year-old underage dumbbell, had not asked for money, only his approval of a plan to make money, to go to college.

Mommy stood up. The mending was done. She knew I was done.

Daddy slipped on his jacket and shot ridicule at me from derisive eyes. "Ha, ha, ha!" he trailed as he left the room, left the house, left me in the lurch. Mommy showed no reaction to my Daddy plea or to Daddy's grim reaction.

She walked out of the room without a word.

I thought it would be better to be a street person, a runaway, or, best of all, a suicide.

Chapter Thirty-Three
Book Madness

I became a covert. Yes, on that day. Yes, feeling so rotten that I had to break a rule and not get caught. Yes, I was a sick girl, defeated by Daddy, and demoted at school. I wanted to become some form of a female James Bond, full of stealth and surreptitiousness and, above all, strength.

I needed to prove to myself that I could rebel, do something forbidden.

Books, I had to be around books or die from wanting books.

I was a book junkie who needed a jab.

I also had an unquenchable desire to hang around a college campus where I didn't belong. I needed recovery time from the Dean scene. I pretended that the book world was where I belonged and that breaking rules weren't a mortal sin.

Thievery didn't interest me. I wanted to crash a party where I wasn't invited, a party where books dominated vast rooms, too many rooms to count, rooms that were designed for the privileged. That would mean I'd be where Daddy told me I'd never be.

I ditched the school bus. I walked to my destination on the awful day that the Dean underscored my dumbbell image so profoundly, in italics. I walked, unauthorized, into the world-famous Widener Library that belonged to the most prestigious college in the world, Harvard.

I flew up the long flight of entry steps, whipped past the classic white fluted columns, Persian in origin and too many to count, and stepped into a massive open space that I knew harbored 3.5 million books. I didn't belong there. This was private property.

Harvard had territorial rights.

I had a territorial imperative.

I had to lose myself among its books. If I got caught so what? So I'd get burned, so what? I knew all about burn.

Feigning Brahmin confidence, I imitated the typical Radcliffe girl. Exuding assertiveness, I walked past the librarian station. No one stopped me. No one asked for identification. The security force within the library was also decidedly disinterested. The curators alternately stood or half-sat on the edge of high stools while helping real students.

I strolled past all of them. I belonged there. That's what I told myself.

This was the boldest make-believe move I'd ever made in my life. I was lying. I shouldn't be lying. But lying about my reality felt so good. So far, I was only lying to myself.

I walked into the first big open space stretched before me. It turned out to be the law section. I put my schoolbag at a vacant place on one of the long tables lit by a series of soothing lamps glassed in green. I'd never thought of green as psychologically calming or aristocratic or a way to enhance a person's focus.

It was all those things, and the library's green light, just like green traffic lights, gave me the confidence to move ahead. This was my Daddy rebellion, my Daddy mutiny, my Daddy uprising.

I looked around, got my bearings.

I was in the section housing floor-to-ceiling rows of leather-bound law books. Ladders on wheels, which I'd never seen, made books stacked on shelves near the ceiling accessible. I liked theoretical rises, not a ladder climb. I reached for a book on the shelf closest to me, at eye level.

My book fantasy had begun.

For a few hours, maybe it was longer, I played a researcher. The book I'd chosen randomly, the weight of a small encyclopedia, was one of a large set of law books about divorce cases involving the division of property. The coincidence of that subject, or that particular book landing in my hands, still amazes me.

I made notes. I did cross-references. I picked out key phrases, the ones that made sense. I pretended I was writing a college thesis. I was having a mad, mad book fling when I should be scrubbing, ironing, or washing. This kind of bad felt good.

One day, or someday, I'd research my stories just like this. I'd research the worlds of literature and art. I'd bury myself in books. I would create dossiers for important interviews, prepare strategies to get quotes no one else could elicit.

I pretended I was a paralegal or a detective on a fact-finding mission. I was doing what writers do. Gathering facts to integrate into a story. I was practicing how to be a journalist, a writer.

This was all make-believe, a daydream, an illusion in a book palace.

Still, no one questioned me. I was happy pretending that I had access to books, any kind of books. I pretended that I'd find a way, somehow, to be a bookish artist lady for the rest of my real life.

In my high school the one about to end, I had crossed paths with two encouragers, one of whom was sincere.

Dumbbell

My junior year English teacher, a man who could have been a Brooks Brothers model, gave me a list of classic literary books to read over the summer, classics to prepare me for college.

In unrelated spurts of free time, even late at night, using a small flashlight, I read every line of every book. I wrote extensive essays. I pretended I was writing them at the Widener, but it was in my room, propped up in bed, after midnight. My English teacher, Mr. Burns, believed I had a future. He graded my papers, all "A's." He told me to follow my ambitions. He said that I had the "right stuff."

There were no burns from Mr. Burns.

My art teacher, a lecher, brushed his hands across my breasts and signed his name to a watercolor landscape I'd just finished. "You're almost as good as me," he said enviously before adding, "and if you tell anyone I touched you, no one will believe you."

Inappropriate touching didn't have a name then. What he'd done constituted sexual harassment. The teacher who signed his name to my work broke another law, plagiarism. These were my first lessons in confronting men with motives, good and not so good, outside the home.

As I walked out of the Widener, darted down the steps, I knew I'd never return. I spoke to that building, a magnificent edifice, as if it were human.

"Goodbye, Widener," I said. "Someday, when I'm a professional writer, you'll invite me back so I can forget that I was an outsider the first time around. I don't want to be an outsider. '

I talked to the formidable Widener, an architectural masterpiece, but I was also chatting with my severely wounded self.

I wasn't sorry that I'd snuck in. I wasn't sorry that I'd ignored the guards who ignored me. I needed a reprieve. I played among the books, bathed in a green light, the way Frank Sinatra played among the stars.

Chapter Thirty-Four
Finals

Daddy made a second devastating telephone call to the Dean.

It was March. Graduation was in June. Daddy ordered me yanked out of high school immediately to go to work in a stockroom. The same Dean delivered this catastrophic blow. She softened the bad news with good news. Both my College Course and Commercial Course marks were high enough for me to graduate with my class. "With honors," she said in a casual aside.

I was speechless. Daddy had rights. I didn't have any rights. The Dean offered no alternatives. Nothing. I was bereft of rights. My high school records, sketchy now, were no longer prospective college credentials. They endorsed the dumbbell theory. I graduated with basic business skills. No longer was I college material.

I had drifted down from college to commercial to nil.

I thought of myself as being dishonorably discharged

from high school. It certainly looked like expulsion to everyone who watched my final exit. And everyone did. I hadn't broken any school rules. I hadn't committed any offense. But Daddy had me kicked out of school, banned me from school as if I'd violated some important mandate.

The cruel departure couldn't have happened at a worse time. The school bell rang. Hordes of students were busy jangling their lockers, exchanging books for upcoming classes, and chatting loudly.

I, on the other hand, was emptying my locker of its entire contents. It was as if I'd been shoved, lunged into the throes of a savaged life not of my own making.

My sudden departure must have looked like plain old expulsion to what seemed like millions of intrusive students thronging around and beyond me.

Gossip about my obvious retreat started with one whisper and zoomed across the big locker room like a wire on fire. Look! She's cleaning out her locker! What did she do? She's being dismissed! No, she's being expelled! She must have done something bad!

My emotions had been stripped bare before but never before an audience of busybodies, my peers.

The rapid buzz-buzz, I heard every syllable, pushed me into an emotional stupor. I felt stigmatized. What was left of my dignity was gone. Daddy's knockout punch left me woozy, dazed. I managed to clean out my locker just as another bell rang, and everyone else headed for his or her next class.

I felt alone and lonely. I burned. The burn was bad. I was bad.

Finally, moving down the empty high school corridors on automatic, headed toward the exit doors for the last time, a blur of disbelief gnawed at me. I managed to get the bus home. I couldn't contact my 1,000 angels. They weren't accessible. I wondered if they existed. I know about desertion. Mommy deserted me. Maybe the angels, 1,000 of them, were deserters too.

Graduation rolled around. Mommy attended the ceremony alone. When I had my diploma in hand, she announced that particular document would be my highest academic achievement, so get used to it.

"Who said so?" I asked boldly, guessing she was probably right.

Her gaze was absent-minded. "Daddy," she said simply.

Chapter Thirty-Five
Career

All I had was the address. Nothing else.

Daddy had scribbled the flimsy information that launched my new life with a fine pen on the back of a used envelope. Mommy handed it to me without a word. The job, pre-arranged and confirmed by Daddy, was a dirty job, far dirtier than my household duties.

That pleased him. He knew what he was getting me into.

I soon learned the department employees in surrounding offices of the government center facetiously called it The Noise Room. It was an airless, windowless, and stinky stockroom turned into a miniature factory. When the two antique iron machines, big, were in full blast, they vibrated, groaned ear-splitting bang-bang-bangs. The smell was god-awful,

I'd been condemned to forever silence at home. Now I was condemned to The Noise Room. The jangling rackets made my head ache. Once I'd pretended to be deaf. Now I was going deaf. I was breathing in bad air. My throat was sore.

My specific job was to use a rag doused in a smelly chemical to clean and then file small addressograph plates alphabetically in old metal cabinets. I asked for rubber gloves. I was told they weren't in the budget. The chemicals saturating the plates, which looked like dog tags, ate the epidermis of my hands faster than the steel wool I'd used to clean our old oven. Sometimes my hands bled. My soul bled too.

Those addressograph plates were a central part of that grubby room.

They were small metal rectangles inserted by the boss's hand into those wretched rickety-rackety machines that printed addresses on envelopes for mass mailings.

The other part of my job was to fold the inserts and stuff them into those envelopes with just-printed addresses. The sealed envelopes were then thrust into large burlap bags.

I was a slim girl not a muscled gym goddess. The work was cumbersome. My back ached. I was working in the facsimile of a small crowded factory.

An unshaven, unwashed, overweight giant wearing raggedy clothes arrived periodically with a dolly, one of those unpowered wagon-like vehicles that move things from one place to another. His job was to haul filled bags of mail to a post office housed in the same building.

I asked the man's name. I wanted to say hello and thank you.

Salvatore, the boss, a few inches short of being a midget, told me to mind my own business. I didn't ask why. Silence was second nature to me.

When I was quiet for a long time, he volunteered the information.

The burly man who took the burlap bags had no tongue. Some maniac had cut it out during a gang fight.

I didn't know if this was true. What danced on my

brain was the thought that he used scare tactics, like Daddy.

I still said "thank you" every time he took a load of the burlap bags I had filled. I had assimilated Mommy's good manners. He smiled, a sort of sardonic half-smile, and I saw he had no teeth. "Someone knocked his teeth out too," Salvatore, informed me when he'd left.

I went home exhausted, headachy, and feeling ill. The sight of food made the nausea worse. All I wanted to do is sleep. I had gotten pencil-thin. That gave me dimples and a tiny waist. It also brought out my high cheekbones. I had "developed," Mommy mumbled, meaning the dumbbell had become a woman.

I didn't care what anybody said. What frightened me was the possibility of a fire in close quarters that housed flammable chemicals. Salvatore smoked. I didn't want to burn to death.

A different kind of fire had already started. An inner fire.

It was in that polluted room that I learned about being a young woman working alongside two lechers in close quarters. Salvatore turned his back to the door, the only door, and looked at me slyly and licked his lips.

He was always trying to push me out of his way when I wasn't in his way. His grimy hands, stained with ink, liked to wander briefly but expertly, across my new curves, as if by accident. He never excused himself. He had molestation on his mind. His eyes were carnal with wanting. It was as if I was there for the taking.

When I said "thank you" to the burlap man, he stared at Salvatore in such a smutty way that I knew they'd planned to join forces when and if they could. There was no one in whom I could confide.

The dark stockroom was a dangerous place. I boxed myself back into my most familiar hiding place: silence. I did my job. I stayed in the open as much as possible. An ordinary please or thank you in this environment was considered overt flirting. That posed rape risks. I was careful to be businesslike, stick to the routine, follow my rule of efficiency without familiarity.

When I got my first little paycheck, $28, I was a little happy. I was working against my will, doing a form of manual labor that Daddy found agreeable, but there, in my hand, were a few dollars.

I felt a twinge of hope. I hatched a little plan.

I couldn't think big anymore. I lowered my expectations substantially. My dollars would go into in a savings account. The department had a credit union. I would put most of my earnings there. It would take a long, long time to earn enough money to go to college at night. I would be patient.

If only I could find my 1,000 angels. They would teach me forbearance.

I had my precious first check in hand, staring down at it, when Mommy slipped by, grabbed it, and walked off. Oh, this was burn. I hated burn. I wanted to run after her, snatch my check back, and insist it was mine. I didn't. Daddy was home. Silence ruled. She was Daddy's cohort.

Later, when Mommy and I were alone, she told me that she'd let me have a "slight" portion of my check back. She didn't say how much. She didn't offer any information as where the other portion, the major dollars, was going.

Mommy had changed radically after The Reverend's warnings, after the lawyer's proposal. She had acclimated herself to Daddy's ways, become more like him in attitude. I asked for my paycheck back. I spoke humbly, out of humiliation. Mommy snapped back sharply that it had been deposited in a secret bank for other purposes.

What? What?

Mommy, seeing pitiful question marks in my eyes, gave me cash. Five dollars.

That was it. Five dollars for a week's work.

I went to the medicine cabinet. I looked for the bottle of iodine. It would be so easy to chuck the iodine down in one big gulp. I wanted to die.

The iodine bottle was gone. The nail poison was gone too. Stuck underneath my nails were traces of the black ink that tasted so awful that I didn't bite my nails anymore.

I needed iodine.

I was very lucky at finding coins on the street. I was always looking down. I'd horde the small change, mostly pennies, and buy a small bottle of iodine that I'd swallow in big gulps. I didn't want to botch my suicide. Daddy had stooped very low to destroy me. I would destroy myself in one fell swoop.

I wondered if Mommy would miss me.

Chapter Thirty-Six
The Root of Evil

Daddy called in political favors.

Nicholas had been admitted into a high-priced prestigious Ivy League college that Daddy claimed he could not afford. I was required to make a financial sacrifice for Nicholas's education while being denied my own chances.

I had no chances. I would never have a chance. Nicholas was male, an adopted son, and I, the dumbbell daughter, had to put her money toward his college education.

Mommy hadn't made that clear when she seized my check. Now I knew the terrible truth about my hard-earned money. It wasn't mine. It was for Nicholas.

He lived on campus. He had heavy expenses. Nicholas was an important fraternity brother, a leader. His dues, which included meals, were exorbitant. He did not work during the school year. When his living expenses became prohibitive, Daddy paid clandestinely. He always had expendable cash stashed away in secret accounts in secret places.

What rankled me is that although Daddy had no trouble scraping together money for Nicholas's education, he considered it his God-given right to dip, at will, into my paycheck to subsidize his son's expenses.

Daddy's self-image of absolute male superiority accelerated since Nicholas's success became his main focus. By helping himself to my paycheck, by putting it toward Nicholas' education, he'd rendered me more helpless than ever.

Daddy loved playing god with God's lesser beings, females.

One of his most basic forms of destruction was to rule his women meaningless by rendering them penniless. If he and Mommy had a disagreement, money for food and household expenses were withheld.

Without any means, a person becomes impotent. Ask any street person. No, ask me. My paycheck was not my paycheck. Emotional abuse had extended into practical abuse. I found Daddy's stymieing methods deplorable.

Rebellion rose in me. I tasted the bitterness of my own bile.

I envied politicians, or anybody, who knew how and when to dissent to get your way. I knew nothing about making a blueprint of, how to make things work in your favor. Somehow I had to find a way to defy Daddy without his noticing. I was too much of a pushover.

If stopping Daddy meant being underhanded, I'd do cagey things.

I wanted to change. I thought I wasn't making good use of my energy.

I had to gamble on myself, be more impulsive. I had to take risks. I had to experiment with becoming another version of me.

I had to replace the battered me with a more effective me.

Long ago, the angels urged me to turn things around,

see what's on the other side. I had to defy Daddy without appearing defiant. Resistance had its own innate dangers. Daddy's early threats remained a reality.

If I rebelled, it would have to be soft rebellion, the kind of subtle insubordination that would escape Daddy's notice.

Guts. I had to demonstrate that I had guts.

Chapter Thirty-Seven
Beginning

Within a week, I was enrolled in two University evening classes.

I saw an amazing newspaper ad written, I thought, just for me. I applied for admittance and was accepted. I paid for tuition in small monthly segments, one semester at a time. I signed up for two courses, journalism and art history. I was in heaven.

I'd found a way to circumvent Daddy, dodge him. I was happily savoring the ability to stand on my own two feet using only leftovers from my hoarded paycheck.

I had twenty cents for supper, tea and toast, at a neighborhood diner. The miserly meal didn't matter. Skimping on food made me look more and more like an anorexic fashion model. Besides, I was the rare "she" in discounted classes geared for male veterans on the G.I. bill who came to the night lectures in droves. I liked competing with ambitious men.

When my journalism grades were among the highest, I was jubilant. My professors, all male, encouraged me.

One professor asked to speak to me immediately after class.

He told me that top editors of local newspapers within the state were asking for his best students to do freelance reporting in the city, $10 a story, with pending deadlines. "Could you manage the full-time stockroom job, handle your classes, and take on a second job too?"

I must have seemed very cool to the idea, but inside I was jumping for joy. If this happened, I could earn more money. I could take more classes and pay in full upfront. I was counting my chickens before they were hatched.

I didn't reply fast enough.

He thought my hesitation, my silence, meant disinterest.

"Think about it" he prompted. His tone was solicitous.

Evening classes were a great hiding place from Daddy. But I couldn't really hide.

Daddy was a formidable enemy. He had spies everywhere. Mommy was one of them. All I could do in night school is forget my real life, listen, and learn, visualize myself becoming the professional I wanted to be.

I thought the burden that I carried to go to night school after a full day's work in the stockroom, on my own penny, would be the heaviest load I'd ever have to carry. I didn't know that Daddy's "putty" theory, the one about "using" me, was looming.

Like most chauvinists, Daddy was a manipulative narcissist. He liked using a third party to do his dirty work. Daddy must have strong-armed the details of my evening absences out of Mommy. My privacy was invaded. I made a mistake. I shouldn't have shared the suggested freelance opportunity with Mommy. She told Daddy everything.

Daddy quickly concocted a clever counter-offensive to what he called my "evening adventures." I'd sidestepped him, an act he considered punishable by abuse heaped on abuse.

His strategy pleased Mommy because it included Mommy.

It was she who delivered the bad news with a clarity I'd never seen before. This must be the Mommy who saw herself as a Wall Street success, the Mommy who spoke reams of personal information to the lawyer man who'd disappeared into thin air.

Chapter Thirty-Eight
Two For Tea

Mommy invited me to tea. This was a first. My heart sunk.

What made me leery is that her attitude was too tranquil to be true. I thought she'd been drugged.

When I'd been cleaning the kitchen shelves a few days earlier, I found an open bottle of Bacardi rum stashed in a dim cupboard corner. In Daddy's handwriting, scribbled in Sharpie across the label, was Mommy's first name. What seemed like an intimate gesture suggested a conspiracy.

Mommy had taken a nip or two. The bottle was half gone. Maybe she was high on the stuff now. She oozed confidence. She set the scene with uncommon civility. Two mugs. Two teabags. Mommy seemed to be in another world, another sphere, and, wherever she was, I was expected to join her.

"Now," she said pouring boiling water from the kettle into our mugs with teabags on a string, "I have news."

This was not going to be one of her nervous rat-a-tat rambles. Mommy did not have the shakes. This was rare. She acted like a woman in absolute control. That was even rarer. And she certainly didn't mince words.

"Your father bought a house today," was her opening bombshell.

I was stupefied and speechless.

"Did Daddy hit the lottery?" I reacted foolishly.

My head spun with a new anxiety. I didn't know why. Mommy remained expressionless, stayed on track. "He put a down-payment on it," she continued nonchalantly. "I sold the pearls and some of my diamond jewelry. I had a 'little' rainy day money put aside. He used that too. "

When Mommy referenced her rainy-day money, I stifled a scream.

She was speaking as if every day wasn't a rainy day, as if the "little" money in her possession wasn't a big chip off my little salary, my tuition, and me. When I was a little lost girl, always hiding, always stuck in silence, I developed a keen sense of transparency. I could sense what was not being said. I sat still now. I was waiting for my insignificant little world to erupt.

It did.

Mommy had bombs and she detonated them, one after the other, to expose and explore the tiny space I'd made for myself in night school, in the outside world.

"You could take two jobs, the stockroom, and the freelance job offered by your professor," she said plainly before dropping the next bomb. "That would produce two paychecks to help pay for our new house."

All these years, Daddy, a natural demolisher, had proclaimed that I was putty. Mommy had just defined dumbbell putty according to Daddy. Now it was all out in the open.

I saw a blinding light flare and burn. I felt lots of burn.

I was to work two jobs and give Daddy my pay from both occupations for a house I didn't want and had never seen.

This shockwave was a new kind of shackle. It made me dizzy with disbelief. Mommy had become Daddy's messenger. I never understood how two married people in severe contention, could ultimately act as one.

"Daddy put the house in your name," Mommy continued. "It's done."

Her half-smile was smudged with guilt as she delivered the punch line: "And, oh, it's a twenty-year mortgage."

Mommy just burned me.

I didn't move because I couldn't move.

My muscles, all of them, were in spasm. Flames licked my wounds.

I stared at Mommy, my sometimes-ally. I'd just lost her. I'd just lost me.

Daddy had robbed me of everything. It started with my name, my soul, my dictionary, my doggie, my voice, my freedom, my spirit, and now he was taking my schooling. Two jobs and night classes too? I didn't need the iodine. I was going to die of exhaustion.

Mommy had not spoken in fast phrases. There were no incomplete sentences left hanging. She was neither high-strung nor abrupt. Mommy, who could assume a killer streak, was all business and deadly calm. It was as if she'd rehearsed this before Daddy made her his destroyer.

I went nuts sitting still, a teenager in siege. I talked to myself. This was a disaster. Defend yourself.

But how can a wounded soldier like me, someone splayed on the ground, stop an enemy, Mommy, from taking more shots?

I studied the beautiful marksman. Mommy was on something and onto something. She'd spoken like an executive giving precise instructions from which there would be no deviations. I'd never seen her so poised, so cold.

She even left tiny spaces of air between her statements to allow the specifics of her "news," to sink in, bit by bit.

When she told the lawyer man she wanted to be as a Wall Street executive, this was probably the way she would have fired an innocent party, heartlessly.

I stiffened. My heart thumped. I couldn't keep my dread at bay. This was treachery. Drinking iodine would have been easier, more complete, than death by a new version of money laundering within the family circle.

I'd just lost Mommy, my sometimes-ally of long ago. She was playing me for a fool. She delivered the punch line, the final blow, with ease.

"Daddy put the house in your name," Mommy revealed, "It's done."

We locked glances. She looked away before I did. She studied her tea, swirled it with a fancy English antique silver teaspoon Daddy had recently given her. Mommy liked good silver the way she liked graduated pearls.

She didn't care a hoot about my night school classes.

She didn't care about my energy, my health, my spirit, my hopes.

She didn't care about me. She'd always said she didn't want me. I believed she stayed with Daddy not to lose me. Now she was throwing me to the wolves and, it appeared, with a certain amount of diabolical pleasure.

"Nicholas wants to run for a Congressional seat," is how she broke the stunning silence between us. "We can't ask him to contribute," she said gently about her only son. "He has personal expenses."

Nicholas was in on this despicable scheme. I was already very jealous of him. Mommy defended him. Daddy adored him. And then there was me, the helpless earner expected to make money and give it away.

"What?" I said bitterly, wishing I could play deaf again. "How could all this happen behind my back? How could Daddy, with you at his side, chain me, by name, to a twenty-year mortgage?"

I took three deep breaths. My voice broke. I recovered myself. Mommy said nothing.

"Twenty years! You're telling me you want me to be a dirt-poor stockroom worker and a struggling freelance writer for twenty years?"

I was out of my mind with the duplicity and treachery hitting me.

"You've betrayed me," I burst out.

I cringed at what Mommy was relating to me. I hated Mommy for agreeing to trample my world, my dreams until what I'd just begun was reduced to zero. She dropped the final kicker, the final focus of this awful tea for two.

"If anything happens," she was saying with cold satisfaction "you alone are responsible for the total payments."

My mind was vacant.

I was being burned alive in the real estate market. The shell of me turned to dust.

Mommy had metamorphosed into someone I didn't recognize.

It was too late for resistance, for meaningful opposition or, what I wanted, a way to break away from this new and unexpected cruel and unusual form of financial imprisonment. I was putty.

"That means you will have added expenses, regularly," Mommy resumed.

A deep silence fell between us again.

It was not the obligatory "Daddy silence."

It was the electrifying silence of hearing your own execution, a death knell by lack of money by starvation, by fatigue. Two jobs and night school too? And the wages grabbed for a mortgage I didn't want?

Defeat gnawed at me. Tea and toast dinners were good. But they were never enough. I always wanted seconds. That's what this gnawing felt like, major hunger pangs left unabated until you starved.

Freelancing for newspapers was about as secure as writing a debut novel without a devoted agent cheering you on. Freelancing was like whistling in the dark or walking a tight wire with no training. My potential wages were whimsical, at best.

I was already without adequate means. I had a rotten full-time job alongside two threatening male fools. And now I was expected to take a second job, still vague, in order to be financially responsible for a house?

I wanted my journalism classes. I needed them. I would not abandon them. But I remember Daddy's brutal huffs, that a girl and books were a dangerous combination. What he wanted from me were two paychecks, no books. The rest of my life would be run on Daddy's terms, not mine.

He'd made me his slave. I was mired in defeat.

I understood now that Nicholas's "A" paper, written roguishly on impulse, was Daddy's final straw. Nobody crosses Daddy, even unintentionally. He had exerted extreme revenge.

A purchase of this magnitude, a house, should not be expected of a teenager with good grades and good dreams, a girl plucked from high school and plunked down in a perilous workroom ruled by madmen with maddening machines.

Daddy should have bought Mommy the house. He was shucking his responsibilities, laying them on me

I hadn't touched the tea.

It was cold.

I was cold.

"The papers are drawn at the bank," Mommy was saying I felt as if she was now delighted to kill the baby she never wanted in the first place.

"Daddy had a lawyer approve them, everything has been cleared," she added.

I was shocked at the contentment in her tone.

"All you have to do is go to the bank with me tomorrow, at 9:00 a.m., and sign the papers," Mommy said. "Your father is too busy."

Daddy had finally broken me. Not punctured me. Not bruised me. I was a broken teenager, burned to a crisp, the parts of me scattered helter-skelter.

The appalling reality of my real name, not the disgusting "dumbbell" name Daddy had hoisted on me, was already typed on a 20-year mortgage waiting for my signature.

Besides, this mortgage had potential legal complications. I did not speak legalese.

What if I found myself in debt, unable to meet the mortgage payments?

One slip on one freelance assignment could be the end. The newspaper world is not known for its mercy. What if I couldn't hold onto the awful stockroom job? What if foreclosure became a threat? The house would be auctioned or possessed by the bank.

And it would be my entire fault.

I did not want the house. I did not want to be saddled with real estate that plucked everything from my wallet.

My heart and my mind were born to be creative. I wanted to invest in my classes, my books, my paints, and my future.

Daddy loved Nicholas with an intensity that equaled his hate of me. Nicholas, now an Ivy League graduate with a degree in Political Science that I helped to bankroll, was salaried. He was free to pursue a career in Washington politics. No mortgage problems for him.

It didn't sound like my voice. It was.

As evenly as Mommy had spoken to me, I mustered, "I don't want to do this."

Mommy sipped the last of her tea. She said what she'd come to say. Silence.

My protest wasn't nearly sharp enough. I hurt so much I wanted to howl. Mommy stared into space when I questioned this abuse: "How could you and Daddy make such a crucial decision involving me, everything about me, without talking to me first?"

I was drained. My voice didn't sound like me.

"How could you confer with a lawyer, a banker, and

settle on a house I know nothing about?"

Mommy sat in that unrelenting destructive silence, leaden. I wanted to throw the remainder of my cold tea in Mommy's face. I'd become motionless. Even strait-jacketed I felt burned. It was the burn, the shock of it, that pushed me back to reality.

"How dare you hit me with a twenty-year mortgage with no warning, without my permission?"

My dissent fell on pretend-deaf ears like the ones I'd assumed long ago. I'd paid mightily for playing deaf. I lost Teddy. Now I was in the process of losing myself. With more stubbornness that I thought I had, I continued my inconsequential rampage.

"After you and Daddy yanked me out of high school, you told me I'd find a way, my way, to attend some form of college without asking you or Daddy for assistance. Remember?"

Mommy's silence was resolute. She pretended to remember nothing.

That didn't stop me from wanting to stop her.

"Once I said *nice guys finish last*, and you came back with *nice guys finish at last*," I said before my voice broke.

She remembered. I caught a glint in her eyes before it disappeared.

I used to think that her "at last" retort represented a kind of truce between us, an understanding *that reaching my goals would take time, be delayed a little. I had accepted that constraint. I'd never considered that one day, in one moment Mommy would whip me with a giant restriction that stole everything from me.*

Mommy's silence was deafening. I continued to rant.

"How could you let me struggle with an awful stockroom job and hoist on me the hardest way to learn things at night, when I'm exhausted? How could you buy a house in my name under these circumstances?"

My voice was a little girl's voice, the broken-hearted Teddy voice of my tenth year. "You're strangling me with a financial responsibility that I can't carry.

"I won't sign," I pledged. "You can't make me sign."

Mommy held up her full palm near my face.

"Stop!" she ordered. "It's done. Tomorrow morning you'll sign."

She left the table, left our tea-for-two that came with devastating freight I couldn't possibly carry. Mommy left me limp.

That night I couldn't sleep. I cursed my fate. I pondered how I could possibly do two jobs and go to college at night. I'd just been ordered by Mommy to pull off a triple play, unassisted. All Daddy wanted from me were my pathetic earnings.

I'd just turned eighteen years old. I paid taxes. Mommy had probably riffled through my shabby old miniature child's desk, found copies of my tax receipts.

A banker friend, someone Daddy probably rewarded secretly, must have made a quick and sly mortgage deal using my name without my knowledge. Too often I'd heard Daddy say to Mommy: "Someday the dumbbell will be useful." Or, too often: "She is putty."

The clandestine day arrived. I was a useful girl made of putty.

An efficient banker, a woman, was waiting for my arrival. The only things on her polished mahogany desk were a leather-bound blotter, new, and sitting on it the pile of legal papers ready for me to sign.

She was standing, checking me out, a skinny teenager who should not be in a commercial bank signing a substantial home mortgage.

She did not acknowledge me by name. She probably knew everything there was to know about my situation. She glanced at Mommy and handed me a pen. I was not treated with the normal hospitality given to a male homebuyer. She did not ask me to sit.

I bent over. My hand shook. I signed what I didn't want to sign.

The clincher came to me the night before.

While in my little bed, under the same old quilt, I faced up to an immense desire, a haunting, that I'd cherished much too long.

What if I could prove to Mommy that the baby she didn't want could become a worthy young woman who'd carry this financial burden with dignity? I'd always ached for Mommy's approval. It was a constant obsession that grew stronger every time she pushed me away.

Obsessions are not subject to reason. I was obsessed with pleasing Mommy.

That night I did what I always did when I was crushed beyond repair. I played with words. On a piece of scrap paper, I wrote the word "worthy" a million times.

The constant scribbling revealed a conundrum.

Worth, as in dollars, is how Daddy measured me. Worthy, as in being worthy, was my focus. I put the thought together. I would be a worthy person who could accumulate worth. I had to recreate my own reality out of nothing, without ending up penniless.

I bit my nails. I pulled my hair. I was like that ten-year-old begging for the return of her doggie. How could I accomplish this impossible turn of events?

A whispery voice from somewhere, nowhere, cemented a thought in my rattled brain. "You're going to find a way." It was angel power making a prediction. I trusted the angels. They could lessen, even erase, my nagging anxieties. I felt calmer. I believed them because I wanted desperately to believe them. Then they were gone.

Iodine wasn't the answer.

That's why I told Mommy, in front of the banker, my witness, that I was doing this to honor her. There was no response from either of them.

I had taken the high road. I'd never felt lower.

The angels weren't in the bank.

Chapter Thirty-Nine
Visitors

The only light shone from a little brass antique lamp next to my bed. My eyes were blurry. A fog surrounded me. I felt marooned. I was facing another momentous crisis alone.

My 1,000 angels emerged, slow motion, out of the night haze, a fuzzy glob gliding effortlessly through walls, windows, and doors, any obstacle, to reach me.

Filled with melancholy, I'd been scribbling in a small notebook the word, "alone," over and over. I was too depressed, too burdened. I couldn't rid myself of the clinging remnants of my abuses added to this new one: the house.

The angels knew that if I didn't turn my thinking around, my whole life would be stuck in hopelessness. I was in serious emotional and financial crisis. I had to face the truth of me, to access what untapped energies lay inside me. Or else I'd become a lost soul who'd slipped through the cracks.

"You are not alone," they hummed again in pleasant musical harmony.

Their consonance, so cordial, subdued me.

The angels had already identified my biggest worries. I had to stretch time, expand minutes into hours. I had to launch an unconfirmed freelance writing job, keep the loathsome stockroom job, attend night school, and retain good grades.

How could I juggle all three? And all that housework dumped on me too? No human had ever cheered me on. I'd been cut off from social connections of any kind. I was, indeed, alone.

That's why I'd been writing the word alone, contemplating how my chronic loneliness was damaging my resiliency.

I also wrote "OMO," shorthand for "on my own."

I also wrote: "Loneliness begets loneliness. The lonely who are left alone become the forlorn alone. That's the worst kind of alone."

My 1,000 angels had both extrasensory perception and x-ray vision. They heard my thoughts. They read my thoughts. Their response was swift.

"You are not alone," they interjected again and again loudly and clearly.

They must have monitored Mommy's pretentious tea treachery, the obnoxious bank signing, the whole shebang stacked against me.

They saw me as I saw myself. I was Daddy's stooge and Mommy's lackey.

They'd eye-witnessed every sobering detail of my inner chaos, especially Mommy, who'd done Daddy's dirty work with an equanimity I didn't think she possessed.

The angels understood the financial hardship of monthly mortgage payments on this dumbbell's life. They saw that I was under a shroud.

What they wanted from me now was clear thinking, lucidity.

My meandering pangs of despair stood in my way. I had to get a hold on myself.

The angel's subsequent questions were sharply targeted, like in a courtroom, like they were arguing their case, summoning logic to untangle the worst of my spiraling doubts.

"Writing is a solitary occupation, isn't it?" is how one angel introduced the subject.

I didn't respond to the rhetorical question. The answer was obvious.

Patiently, like a shrewd courtroom operative, they made their point another way. 'It's something you do alone. Just like when you paint images," they rephrased.

Yes, yes. The words crossed my mind. I did not say them out loud.

"Your father imposed an incessant solitude on you?"

It ached to go over this again and again. Yes, I thought reluctantly.

"By secluding you, he *excluded* you. Isn't that what you felt, what you feel now? Excluded?"

Yes. My 1,000 angels had the uncanny ability to measure the degree of pain that Daddy's restrictions jammed inside me.

"He thrust isolation and silence on you, left you void of earthly companions."

Yes.

"You are lonely and overwhelmed by the financial destiny that has fallen on you." There was a pause. "You feel yourself in peril."

Yes. Yes.

"That's why you're writing 'alone' and 'OMO.'"

I was lost in angel rhetoric, immersed in it.

When they zeroed in on the specifics of my truth, I realized, with deference, that they were not only soothers. They were profoundly analytical. They could pluck the simple facts out of my mangled complexities. This was brilliant.

The angels proceeded to summarize the inner me like a clever barrister making the final argument to win the case.

"The terrible experience of being sequestered against your will, all that aloneness heaped on you, the too-frequent hushes and shushes, all that blame and responsibility, everything done against you cannot be changed factually," they recapped.

Oh, how the truth burned. Oh, this was the burn of all burners. I did not want to hear that ones history couldn't be altered.

Did the angels mean forever? I hoped not.

I was Daddy's unwilling doormat a puppet on strings that he manipulated. Did the angels mean I could never affect extreme change in my life? Ever?

This heated conversation with the angels, in complete silence, was making me frantic again, pushing me into the kind of frenzy I'd felt when Mommy hit me with a mortgage in my name. I'd gone nuts mulling the mountain of dollars I had to earn and turn over to Daddy, via Mommy, for a house I didn't want to subsidize. Twenty years! That's two decades!

The angels forced me to face myself as I was. Pathetic. I was unable to stand up, tough it out. I was broken, really broken. The angels saw my grief in total. They picked me up. I rose without moving.

Their tone became kinder, more solicitous. Yet their message was intense. They wanted me to be fierce, to become a warrior.

"Your experiences can be turned into advantage," the angels said earnestly, as if vindication was the easiest thing in the world. "You can rectify things."

They saw exoneration. I felt only defeat.

They saw fight. I felt toppled.

I weighed their hurting words first, the ones about not being able to change the past. I'd been trying to change my life all my life.

I pouted. I thought pouty thoughts.

The angels, maybe they weren't "my" angels, after all, were being grossly unfair. How could they present this theory of starting over so carelessly when I'd just been flogged?

I didn't know what they knew: that the intense righteous indignation I was expressing, the kind based on years of insult and injustice, can be a terrific stimulus if, big if, it is properly rechanneled. Frenetic energies like fear and anger are just waiting to be harnessed, waiting to be focused, waiting to be utilized, waiting to be channeled.

They were offering me an incentive to get up, get going.

Still, I resisted the angels. I was perverse.

The angels didn't understand the full extent of the vicious circle that clenched me and clawed me. Complaints zoomed through my brain. I whined about old baggage that followed me wherever I went and, now, these new financial stumbling blocks.

The emotionally abused girl, the bullied me, was talking her heart out without words. The angels heard every pulse of every heart-rending thought.

Watching Mommy's emotional demise bothered me. She needed help. I wanted to help her. She had stayed with Daddy so I wouldn't be kidnapped. I loved her for sacrificing so much. But she had shifted her allegiances, banned me. I ranted about wanting more college. I envied Nicholas. I never used the word "equality." But that's what I wanted, equal opportunity.

I'd already been capsized, shut out.

I told the angels that I'd lost my way. I needed a map. I needed direction. I needed the physical and mental energy to do two jobs and succeed in night school. I was drowning, gasping for breath, gulping water. But in reality, I was in bed, quiet, having this emotionally charged conversation with the angels or, strangely, with myself.

Please help me. Oh, please.

My appeal was pitiful, like me. I didn't know to whom

I was talking or if there were actual listeners in my room.

On the other hand, the angels were evaluating the glum ramblings zooming through my soul faster than I could think them. I paused to take a breath, to grumble even more. They knew. They understood. They needed no more information.

They interrupted my self-doubts with a startling prognostication. "You were born to be a remarkable woman," I heard. "You have two great gifts."

Instantly, using only a twinkle I felt rather than saw, I felt relief. Encouragement, however flimsy, is a remarkable gift to anyone who has been emotionally abused. It feels like stumbling upon an oasis in a vast desert when you're dying of thirst.

Were my angels hinting I was worthwhile, not worthless? I'd love to be seen as a worthy person. I'd been told over and over that I had no value. Did I have value? Was I, the dumbbell, actually a person of merit?

A glimmer of hope sparkled inside me. I grabbed it. I held it in a vise-like grip.

"What gifts?" I beseeched, sounding like a child begging for candy.

"Both gifts are done with your hands," the answer came drifting into my ears. "But you have to match your intelligence to your imagination, balance them. Your two hands are your God-given vehicles, the instruments of your creativity."

Okay, I thought, they're talking about emotional intelligence.

But I need to understand more. I need details.

Angels don't dilly-dally. They slid into my consciousness effortlessly.

"You write with your hands," I heard. "You paint with your hands."

That's as far as the angels got before I started to complain again. I rode the rapids of my abuse issues without a word. They were tuned in. to my ever nuance, every quibble.

"I barely exist in my environs," I said, knowing they were reading me. "Surviving under a storm of emotional abuse which, when sustained on a regular basis, is a killer."

I then said the silliest thing. "I am a dead duck."

They ignored my "killer" comeback. They had infinite patience.

My complaints were getting old. I didn't know how to fix things.

I whined about everything that oppressed me. Whining is only a temporary tranquilizer. You say what bothers you and what bothers you stays put.

"Aloneness, combined with the misery of paying off a mortgage, are the two penances that make you cringe now," is what I heard clearly.

Yes.

"You think of them as levies against you. You think your father made you his slave."

They heard yes, yes, whirling through my brain.

"Turn your punishments around," was their comeback. "Look at them in reverse."

I thought the angels were talking gibberish.

They ignored me. I'd begun to close myself off from them.

"Consider your brave reactions to the issues you've already faced," they resumed, bypassing my resistance. "Don't you see how you've thrived despite them?" They knew I didn't think I'd flourished at all.

Here they took their time.

They wanted the words, two special words, to sink in, remain sunk inside me forever and ever.

"You have already mastered two vital life lessons," they proclaimed. "They are perseverance and persistence."

I heard those words echo back to me like sound waves from a mountain: *Perseverance and persistence.*

My 1,000 angels were talking about tenacity and doggedness. They were referring to my never giving up. They meant try, try again. Be unstoppable.

"Yes," the angels said, weighing my thoughts. "That's it."

I reasoned, or maybe the angels reasoned it for me, that any adventuresome person, anyone who invents something out of nothing, experiences rejection. Being spurned is a reality that is interwoven intricately, if not indelibly, into any creative process. When a pioneer pushes boundaries, it's like breaking rules. Rebellion erupts. So does envy. So does fear of the unknown. Rejection haunts you when fainthearted people can't, or won't, accept originality.

I know this now.

I didn't know this then.

Then I thought: Burn! Creativity involves burn. Writers and artists are subject to harsh criticism. They're pushed aside, even when their work scintillates with beauty. Rejections, in its many jagged forms, are their fate.

Was I, a crushed creative, born to burn?

The answer echoing back to me, surrounding me, beckoning me, absorbing me, was a repeat issued with such power that it played on my mind like the snippet of a song you can't get out of your head.

"Perseverance and Persistence" was the last thing the angels said before I fell sound asleep.

Chapter Forty
Smarts

My first thought upon awakening was strange but very, very true.

When intermingled, the two stunning words, emotional and intelligence are intertwined. You have to be smart about how you tap the power of your feelings.

That thought alone overpowered my imagination. If you aren't in control of your emotions, you become powerless. I was guilty of that my whole life. I'd been in a fog, confounded.

One angel heard my thoughts and declared that miracles snowball from the smallest, most insignificant beginnings.

"You have to take a leap of faith," is what I heard.

"Leaps are dangerous," I countered. "You have no idea where you're going to land. You could kill yourself without iodine."

That angel pretended absolute calmness while the words "iodine" and "suicide" sieved through my brain. Then the words disappeared. The angel eradicated them. Just like that. Pouf.

"You do what you think you can't do," was the conspicuous comeback. "But first you consider all the information at hand, all the possible outcomes, and then you make an intelligent decision about when and where to leap."

I was going to argue with this angel, all the angels, but they interrupted me: "You're wasting your time thinking you're still putty," was the solicitous, phrase prancing in and out of my earlobe."

Still, in spite of all the mentoring, I thought negatively: I am an empty crater. I am burned beyond recognition. I am the shredded fragment of the real me.

The angels heard these negatives slashing what was left of my ego. "All the burnings that came to you in the form of booby traps and minefields, have built up your muscle," an angel, speaking for all the angels, declared.

The words, flipping from puffs of fresh air, stuck to me.

The angels could see the far, far distant future. They wanted me to believe in myself, believe that what lay ahead was doable. I had nothing to lose because I had nothing.

I made a decision.

Instead of falling apart, I'd muster my strengths, make the muscles I'd developed the hard way become assets. I needed punch power. I knew, in my heart, that I had capabilities and energies.

Despite my harsh lessons in survival, I'd survived.

That was hard to admit, very hard. I'd wanted to give up, die, so many times. "You've already proven yourself," was the whisper I heard,

The angels made me realize that all the Daddy deals prepared me for unpredictable career setbacks that come with any professional climb. If I could survive Daddy, I could survive the Daddy types I'd encounter on the job. I'd assembled a lot of emotional missiles. I'd have to figure out how to use them to my advantage.

"That's exactly what emotional intelligence is all about," came at me from somewhere, nowhere "When you're emotionally intelligent, you emit sparks of enthusiasm," the angels said. "Stop being so meek. Let your little light shine. People are drawn to you."

I was in a state of transformation. I laughed. "Meek is weak, isn't it?" I asked.

I heard a ripple of distant laughter mingling closely with mine. That meant yes.

The angels dropped the word, paper, on me.

"Your ambitions have everything to do with paper," they sang out.

It was true.

When I was stuck in uninterrupted silence and isolation, I wrote or painted on paper. If I added emotional intelligence to the equation, my creativity might ignite.

I don't know how I came to this conclusion.

My professor, the one who'd offered me freelance jobs, had already asked if I could tackle assignments on deadline.

Okay, I'd write after midnight. I'd write on nights I had no classes. I'd write on paper napkins available with tea and toast. I'd write on weekends, between class assignments and housework and homework. I'd find a way to hobble into the world of words.

I got a little shaky. This time the angels let me think for myself.

What I faced was grueling. I'd have to take on a series of unrelated writing assignments, please a variety of critical editors, and do everything else expected of me within the same time segment.

The angels tossed golden confetti at me: "You already know you have emotional intelligence. You're going to work things out."

I sensed the angels smiling.

A glob doesn't smile. I felt a smile. I never saw a smile. I never heard a voice. I just thought I *heard* a voice. I never saw wings. I only saw a white circle going 'round and 'round.

Then it burst like a bubble gum bursts. Pop!

Chapter Forty-One
Phoenix Rising

The next night, waiting for my class to organize, I scribbled a note to myself: "Like a phoenix, I will rise from my own ashes. All I need are two jobs." I added the words: "Quick-quick."

My professor asked again to speak to me privately after class. We stood at the door, our backs to the exiting students. He handed me my latest essay, pointed to an "A-plus" with his index finger, and repeated the pivotal question.

Several out-of-town editors had asked him to recommend his best student for freelance assignments. This time he was specific. One editor, a friend of his, requested a student to write a piece on Mrs. Franklin Delano Roosevelt, who was lecturing at Harvard the next day, Saturday. The story would be needed immediately, $10, to begin.

Would I like the job? Would I!

Could I meet the deadline? Could I!

That's how I learned women who have no rights could

earn rights. That was my first inkling that post-Suffragettes, drowning in male dominance and unfair obstructions, became the pre-liberationists who laid the groundwork for Feminism.

I was one of them.

The next thing I knew I was racing past "my" Widener Library, the one I'd raided, ran through one section of the famous Harvard Yard, headed toward the looming red brick building in which Mrs. Franklin Delano Roosevelt was to speak on women's rights. I was on my first assignment for a small regional newspaper on Cape Cod.

I was starting at the top. That's what I told myself.

The spring day was sunny. Tulips and daffodils were blooming everywhere. It was noon. The gentle wind, or was it destiny, whisked me forward, pushed me next to Mrs. Roosevelt, who was walking to her speech alone. Alone! I knew all about alone. She glanced at me and smiled approvingly.

Destiny dotes on perfect timing.

An extemporaneous meeting with The First Lady, both of us moving to the same destination simultaneously, was very unlikely. My 1,000 angels must be whisking around somewhere close.

We walked in tandem. Yesterday I was a wretched eighteen-year-old. Today I was in the company of one of the greatest human rights advocates of the 20th century, a Feminist before the word was coined. We were an unlikely pair.

I introduced my mission and myself as if we were both big-time.

She walked fast, fast, and asked fast, fast, if freelance meant free?

"Ten dollars," I beamed. "I am going to get ten dollars."

"Great!" she said gleefully. *"If you can write you can do anything."*

My soul devoured Mrs. Roosevelt's prediction. It

became my secret mantra, the shield I wore at home, in silence, in classes, in the stockroom, on assignment. They're still a part of me. I want them etched on my tombstone.

I, a mere fledgling reporter, made mental notes as we strode toward our mutual destination. It was a trick I'd learned from my journalism professor, the one who got me this assignment.

"Observe without being observed," he'd advised, not knowing that I'd regularly practiced that handy habit at home and everywhere.

Mrs. Roosevelt did not stroll. She moved like a woman on a mission.

She didn't step out of a limousine. She was on foot, like me. No bodyguards accompanied her. We were worlds apart, yet we shared the commonality of aloneness.

Her windswept French twist hairdo, like Mommy's wedding hairdo, was loosening. Bobby pins were dangling. She didn't care. Her silk dress and matching tunic, was pale pink and wrinkled. It was ordinary ready-to-wear, store-bought. No couturier had dressed her. A funny veiled hat, shaped like a wiggly crown that had a veil, was like those idiotic frou-frou hats still worn by British royalty.

No aide was around to save her from looking unkempt or, in fact, to save her from anything. Alone. She was alone. Her black leather shoes were mannish Oxfords, made for stomping. Cosmetics were not among her interests, not even a slash of light pink lipstick. Her skin was flawless. Photographs never captured her unassuming naturalness or her magnetism, the assets that made her truly lovely.

The historic brick building materialized. The entrance was an oversized planked wooden door. An aristocratic staff waited there to greet Mrs. Roosevelt, who was immediately whisked toward a podium.

Chapter Forty-Two
Taking Notes

The room was filled, every seat taken, standing room only. An usher found a folding chair that he set up in a corner where I could see and hear everything.

I never told Mommy about my Mrs. FDR encounter or how the president's wife predicted victory for me in a way that going to church every Sunday didn't. Mommy would not have believed me anyway. I mentioned that I'd be getting small checks as often as possible for mortgage payments.

"Writing is a poor man's business," Mommy sniveled when I put my first $10 check in her hand.

I forgave her. Daddy had shattered her spirit. She was disjointed.

I wanted to make her whole again, the way she was the first time she confronted Daddy and asked for a divorce. We faced Daddy together, hand-in-hand. She sat oposite him. I stood at her side, our hands wound together in a distinct bond, the loving unity of a mother and a four-year-old daughter.

I thought Mommy was mine forever. She'd hugged me and kissed me just before she asked Daddy for a divorce. She told me that it would be the two of us together always. She was strong then, in her prime. I was an innocent little girl on the verge of emotional destruction. We both were.

But at that moment, facing Daddy together, I vowed to love Mommy truly, always, no matter what. Sad incidents had interrupted that pledge, stomped on it. I was just a little girl who knew nothing about how man-woman relationships can rot and change the course of life. As I grew up, as I saw their marriage disintegrate, I'd secretly wished that Mommy had gotten the divorce she wanted.

And that fateful day, facing Daddy with her, I was too little to understand that emotionally abused women like Mommy have emotionally abused daughters, like me. Once Daddy put impenetrable walls around her, the jailing that changed her, he taught her how to abuse me, break my spirit.

Now Mommy, this changed woman I called Mommy, didn't believe a girl child should be encouraged to write or paint.

But I was doing it anyway. I had perseverance and persistence.

I began to have a string of minor successes, a regular flow of freelance work followed by checks, one after the other. I wrote quickly, confidently, and with a reverence for words.

I'd say to me what the angels had said to me more than once:

"You are finally mining your real self. You have your very own holy place inside you, a sacred vault that no one can access. No one! It's your soul. It's where you house your insights, intuitions, instincts, your talents, everything precious to you."

I began to talk to myself as if I hadn't been broken, as if I was a whole person. I told myself that tools for an ultimate victory were in my possession. I spoke to myself with such insistence, such forcefulness, that I appeared stronger than I was.

My 1,000 angels chimed in from nowhere: "Let no one stop you."

They didn't want me to take any steps backward. There were times when my energy was depleted, when fatigue halted my brain. Coffee, I lived on coffee. That's how I fought off discouragement and surrender. Sometimes I got lost. Sometimes I thought I couldn't succeed big while juggling so many small things at once.

"Don't back away or back down from opportunities," the angels insisted. "You're going to break barriers."

The angels fortified me. What I heard from them was like a power punch of adrenaline more powerful than Mommy on rum.

I reread my Mrs. FDR research, more items I didn't use, items that the newspaper didn't want for lack of space. I began to see that all humans are linked. Class may separate them, but they are all equipped with the same set of emotions. I, a poor teenager, had walked with a First Lady, a revered celebrity. But we both submerged our loneliness in writing.

There was another uncanny connection.

My birth year was 1932.

When my mother spoke of my natural birth at home, she said FDR was on the radio beside the bed, accepting his victory as 32nd president of the United States.

Mommy was already under the influence of a chauvinist husband who'd have affairs outside the marriage. Mrs. FDR produced babies while her husband, the philandering president, had an affair with Lucy Mercer, his wife's friend.

Mrs. Roosevelt had a hellish mother-in-law, a miserable woman who doted on making her miserable. I had five miserable aunts who'd wanted me kidnapped, a child seized from her Mommy.

Mrs. FDR was made to believe she was unattractive, like me.

She was told she could accomplish nothing of importance, like me.

Yet she was the only First Lady to hold regular press conferences for women writers. She wrote a successful syndicated newspaper column while on the run. Someday I'd do that too.

When I was at home, less and less now, doing the chores faster and less fastidiously than I should, the "someday" seemed to be inching closer.

Daddy liked all the extra checks that Mommy passed on to him. Daddy had robbed me of my speaking voice. I let him believe he still owned it and, of course, me. My writing voice was intact. That's what counted.

I heard him say to Mommy: "She has no guts left. Once a dumbbell, always a dumbbell."

Chapter Forty-Three
Forgiveness

Rummaging through the crumbling paper contents of an old hinged wooden box, I found a key.

It was the most extraordinary key I'd ever seen.

The key size was unique. It was not an ordinary door key. It symbolized a key to heaven, history, and heraldry. I was curious. I pulled it out of the box. I was amazed at the purity of its aesthetics.

It was an antique, bigger than my hand, heavy, and made of solid brass. When it was new, it must have shone like pure gold. It hadn't been cleaned in ages, but it still projected an underlining golden hue that reflected gone glories.

My eyes were glued on the intricate open curlicues scrolled at the top of the key. The precise design, a merge of clever twists and intertwined circles, exuded a signature of prestige and power.

Even soiled, embedded with dirt, I was fascinated. I ran

my fingers over ghostly fingerprints from past centuries

"Keep looking," I heard from someone, or something, that shook my musings.

The key looked Edwardian. But I knew it was influenced by classical Greek styles. It was probably designed to open a heavy wrought iron stable gate backing a rich man's mansion. It symbolized horses, a primitive form of transportation.

For me, this found key implied escape.

Emotionally abused girls always harbor nasty twangs of need that never go away. I still thought "escape" meant a physical fleeing to another place. I hadn't yet realized, at least not fully, that words take good writers to unexplored spheres even while they're sitting still, working. And that's the greatest escape of all.

That magnificent key had been laying in wait among Daddy's final belongings.

I was destined to find it.

Mommy had asked me to discard whatever he'd left behind. "I have other things to do," is the way she dismissed me. Caustically. Daddy hadn't left her anything of value.

She began crocheting her fifth magnificent bedspread with an exacting pattern, three-dimensional Roses of Tralee blooming every few inches. I'd glanced at the instruction book. It looked like complicated mathematics. I couldn't fathom it. Mommy was an amazing artist with needles and threads. In the end, the busyness and concentration required of a virtuoso "crocheter" had saved her sanity.

I squatted on the wooden floor, just like I'd squatted on the worn linoleum the awful day Daddy hung me as the dictionary dumbbell. His things were strewn around me.

The small box that hid the key had been nestled within the folds of a rag, a beaten-up bathrobe on the verge of shreds. I found the box stuck in a corner of Daddy's untidy closet. He must have hidden the key and forgotten all about it.

Daddy was superstitious about keys. I'd overheard him

telling Nicholas delightful legends about keys. I'd probably blocked out the best parts, like telling his son that he'd hidden a spectacular antique key among his things.

The uncanny source of one unforgettable myth he'd shared with Nicholas has always stayed with me. It was connected to my birth.

The month of January is named after Janus, the Roman god of keys.

Daddy married Mommy in January. She was pregnant within weeks.

Discovering the antiquated history of Janus and the key, the very one in my hand, was a combined coincidence. Did it contain an esoteric message?

Detailed in an aging encyclopedia, I discovered the most mind-boggling key myth of all: *A gold-colored key symbolizes the ability to open the door of forgiveness.*

I shuddered after I'd read it more than once. What?

If this legend was true, the key had hastily become extremely personal.

I was meant to find this key. And maybe I was meant to forgive.

I reread the vivid encyclopedic passage.

I pondered Forgiveness.

Daddy was dead. I alone was cleaning out his closet and happened upon a splendid key that, according to ancient belief, enabled me to unlock the door to forgiveness?

Who was to forgive whom?

Was I to forgive Daddy or vice versa?

The improbable implication, surely I imagined it, was that Daddy might now be sorry—sorry—sorry that, in life, he had heaped severe and constant emotional abuse on me.

Had destiny put the concealed key in my hand, forcing me to consider that Daddy was sending me an arcane sorry—sorry—sorry message from wherever he was?

I trembled. A puff of fragrant flowery air, jasmine embraced me, and I knew that the angels, now an integral part of me, were saying: "You must forgive him! It'll feel as invigorating as the air you breathe."

So that was it?

It was I who had to forgive Daddy? It was I who had to throw off the grievous memories he'd piled on me, ruining my early life? It was I who found the box, discovered the key, and received the mystical message to forgive.

The angels, surely this were all angel doing, heard me shaking with grief, anger, and this sudden pressure to release my Daddy burden.

"The only way you can mend yourself, feel good about the progress you've made, is to forgive." I heard. "You must rise to the occasion, respect yourself without reservation. The only possibility of resurrecting yourself is to forgive your Daddy for all the emotional whippings you've endured."

Too hard, this was too hard.

Everything about Daddy was hard to reconcile. This was excruciating. He'd flogged my heart and soul. He'd beaten my dreams to nothingness. Daddy was an injurer. I was, still am, the injured party.

The punctures, the pierces he made remain wounds that never healed. I still have them. Look.

Daddy, who'd mangled my spirit, never had a smidgeon of forgiveness in him while he'd lived. Now it was too late. In life, he'd considered himself a blameless authoritarian. He favored revenge and punishment. Yet, in death, in an enigmatic moment, a concealed key exemplifying forgiveness sat in my clenched fist.

The whole weird idea of the exquisite key and its link to my forgiveness was totally insane.

The writer in me, the girl who'd always thrived on her imagination, reminded me that I was a detective who could piece together a puzzle and see the whole picture. That's what writers do.

Yet the illogical me, a girl who'd been beaten to shreds, resisted any thought of forgiveness. Daddy's sins slashed too deeply. That's why I became tongue-tied when, in my eighth decade, the hospital lady floored me by asking if I'd ever been emotionally abused.

But I knew, despite everything, I'd come to a momentous crossroad. Daddy's treasured key marked a milestone intersection in my journey. I gave the key sober thought. It was, for me, the leap of all leaps.

But if I was emotionally intelligent, I could forgive. I should forgive. Forgiveness was the actual "escape" I'd always coveted. I'd free myself from all the bad memories that still plagued me.

I struggled inside. The Daddy memories were embedded deep within me. They defined me. I'd have to rip a part of me away, toss it. With the key still clenched in my hand, I thought darkly: how can you forgive the unforgiveable?

I'd been snared into something supernatural.

"Forgive him!" the angels rammed at me from nowhere, thrusting the two words at me as if they were flying objects. I was shaken by the speed and velocity with which their demand was thrown at me.

Victims don't forgive easily.

Daddy had trespassed on his little girl's life. He'd savaged her feelings. He should have begged my forgiveness before it was too late to broach the subject.

Only now it was too late.

He was sitting alone in a small cafe, drinking coffee, when he tumbled off the stool and crashed to the floor in a heavy heap of nothing. My nemesis was gone.

Somebody called an ambulance.

The young doctor who pronounced him dead at the hospital used colorful language when Mommy asked if Daddy's fatal heart attack was an instant killer. "He probably felt as if he'd been hit by a thousand sledgehammers," he said. "It was acute, thorough, and irreversible."

I tried to feel sorry for Daddy.

I didn't.

Daddy was on the verge of being reduced to dust. I didn't care. If I felt nothing for Daddy in life, how could I forgive him in death?

But I was holding the key, his antique key, and the doctor picked the number, "one thousand," to illustrate how many sledgehammers it took to kill Daddy. I was boggled. I have a thousand angels? And it took a thousand sledgehammers to kill him?

This was not a coincidence.

But what about my doggie, the discarded dictionary, my lost football game, my unused ice skates, my dumbbell status, my cut-off from school, my snatched paychecks, my...

"Stop ruminating," commanded my angels.

Or was that me talking to me?

"Stop reliving the old Daddy scenes over and over. It's finished."

Emotional abuse is never finished. How could the angels lie to me?

"You can't undo what's done," a voice reminded me solemnly. "But you can finish it off by erasing it."

"They don't make those kinds of erasers," I sneered.

"The kind of eraser you need is a portable fire extinguisher that douses fire," the angels retorted. "You have to let the burns go."

I was too young to realize that forgiveness is the ultimate escape. The only escape. It means conceding forever, the hurts that inundate you, obstruct you, hold you back. You have to allow forgiveness to wash over you, cleanse and refresh you, like the magical waters I'd walked on with the angels. You have to drown your burns. All of them.

I stared at the key that supposedly could open the door to forgiveness. I remained defiant. Daddy should have said sorry—sorry—sorry to me. He didn't deserve my forgiveness.

You could say you forgive and, in your heart, not

forgive at all.

You can fake forgiveness. Then it comes back to haunt you.

Forgiveness is a slippery slope. If it's true forgiveness, it involves absoluteness. Once you forgive, forgiveness has to be final. You can't be unforgiving once you forgive.

How could I truly forgive, once and for all, how Daddy had wrecked the child of me, the girl of me, the teenager me?

I put the question out there.

How? Tell me how.

The angels were brutally honest: "The quickest way to forgive, to really forgive, is to do it in one immense stroke," they said. "And you can't look back. Ever. You have to wipe the slate clean, start fresh."

This was much too much to ask.

"If you forgive slowly, you will prolong the agony of letting go," a voice slid in. "Your Daddy isn't here to hurt you anymore."

An abused child fences herself in. She builds walls. Daddy was my oppressor. The angels heard great shards of hostility wrangling inside me.

"The emotionally intelligent person knows that she must walk away from personal disasters or be consumed by them." That was my angel message. "Break down the walls. Unfence yourself."

The angels had never goaded me like this.

They'd never badgered me.

They'd never argued with me so intensely, so logically.

They'd never provoked me with such intensity.

They were hounding me to forgive.

The key. It vibrated in my palm. I felt a slight tremor. It gently pulsed and throbbed. Maybe I'd inherited Mommy's shaky hand

I looked down. The hand holding Daddy's key was still. Was Daddy making a paranormal connection with his dumbbell? Was that even a vague possibility?

I wanted to ditch my feelings of bondage. I needed to be detoxed. I hadn't yet found my true compass. I had no way to measure my capacity to create forgiveness. I was still wrestling to be the ultimate me. The strange key gripped me and I gripped it. We seemed linked.

I told myself that I could not forgive Daddy straight away. The protective wall I'd built around me was terribly isolating. I still felt terribly alone. I still felt the burn,

The angels heard my thinking.

The emotional abuses I'd suffered had to be irrevocably removed like splinters, one by one. I have no idea, none, why I equated all my emotional burns with splinters.

The angels told me why.

"Splinters can cause abscesses inside the body, create life-threatening complications," was the explanation. "Abscesses cause fevers that burn incessantly."

Forgiveness would save me from further burn. Oh, I hated burn.

Without words, I decided to forgive Daddy.

But I had to do it my way.

Chapter Forty-Four
Junking

I gave my burden a name. Trash.

All the emotional abuse I'd endured was trash.

The only way to strip away the old torments, cancel the losses, and quash my severe sense of inferiority was to treat my abuse like disposable garbage.

To save myself, free myself, I had to pluck out each depressing abuse one by one, as if they were splinters ready to abscess

"Stop procrastinating," the angels coaxed vigorously. "Emotional abuse gobbles up your inner self, munches it. This is trash time."

They were right. It was now or never.

The consequences of holding onto emotional ghosts and ghouls can lead to the kind of depression that becomes a lifetime load. It can paralyze you. It can render you directionless and purposeless. It can goad you into believing you have no goals, no energy, no purpose.

Something red-hot shot through me like molten lava.

Strangely, this burn was a nice burn. It warmed me up. It lit up the road in front of me. It reignited the dormant possibilities lurking with me. My dead Daddy didn't murder the best in me after all. I survived. I still had lots of gumption. I was on a self-rescue mission.

It was as if I'd climbed a small mountain without shoes and, standing on a peak, looked down at my trail.

It was in that nasty, stinking stockroom, The Noise Room, that I learned the true meaning of persistence and perseverance.

Day after day, I performed under pressure.

I made good grades in my nighttime courses. Everything I'd learned, I put to good use.

I was a dependable freelancer. Lots of little checks floated my way.

When I was hungry and sleepy, someone offered me coffee. Or if found small change on the streets, I bought hard candy because the sweetness lasted. That's how I assuaged my food cravings.

I was obsessed with my creative goals. That bolstered my courage.

Somehow, don't ask me how, I was instantaneously transported to a fictitious dumpster, a place where I could ditch all my emotional pain, close the lid, and walk away free.

Chapter Forty-Five
Good Riddance

There I was, standing near the dumpster.

I opened the lid and looked inside. It was empty. It seemed to be soliciting junk.

I heard the angels telling me to imagine the fictitious dumpster as the facsimile of a casket, to believe that I was *burying* my abuse like unwanted debris, piece by piece.

I thought, this is warrior work. At last, I am a warrior.

Out of nowhere, the 1,000 angels interjected themselves. Their words drifted into my ears: "To become a real warrior, you have trash your trash! When you eliminate old debris, the real you will surface."

With each specific discard, I became more buoyant. The angels shone their 1,000 watts on what I was trashing. They wanted me to see, and remember, that I'd trashed my trash.

I had to forget forever that I'd been branded a dumbbell.

Trash.

The tomb of silence in which I was trapped, the Daddy curse that made me voiceless and expressionless?

Trash.

My stolen doggie Teddy, the only earthly loyalist I ever had, taken because I played deaf when the loud fights became unbearable?

Trash.

The nasty way Mommy, under Daddy's influence, had propelled Lucille, my friend in music, out of my existence.

Trash.

My hand-made treasure, the tiny palm crown given to me by my favorite nun, Sister Rose, ravaged in front of me without provocation?

Trash.

When Daddy trashed my dictionary, trashed the dinner table, trashed the dining room, trashed my high school life, trashed my college aspirations, and cursed me for being a dumbbell, a "She."

Trash. Trash. Trash.

The no-books for girls decree and the destruction of a long-gone dictionary that gave me my first inkling of what soul is? The surprise demotion followed by the removal from my high school class?

Trash. Trash.

The new house that I was forced to help finance? Trash. My sparse paycheck and miniscule savings geared for my night school studies, handed over for Nicholas's education?

Trash.

My sin for coming into the world unexpectedly and unwanted?

Trash.

The constant kidnap threats, the idea of being orphaned, and given to one of Daddy's sisters, was trash, trash.

I was so nervous trashing that I jumped as if I'd been smacked hard. It was just a gentle shoulder tap of encouragement from the angels. I was too edgy. I had to keep cool.

They insisted that trashing one's trash is the healthiest thing I'd ever done: "It's like showering away the day's dirt and grime but in a much, much bigger scope."

One final doubt refused to loosen its grip.

Could someone like me trash forever the thought that Daddy had trashed me? Could I forget forever I'd been bullied, emotionally abused?

"Yes, you can," I heard in a lovely singsong. "You have a clean slate now."

An ocean materialized out of nowhere.

The dumpster or casket, whatever it was, seemed weightless. I pushed it into the water. It bobbed for a split second before being drowned by a gigantic wave. The next thing I knew, I was playing in the water, riding the breakers like a surfer without a surfboard.

The angels were doing the same thing.

Everywhere I looked I saw 1,000 globs, walking on water, dancing on water, or rolling in the swells of the water.

Either they had joined me, or I had joined them.

We were doing the same things in the same place at the same time.

Chapter Forty-Six
Communiqués

I pondered how the angels messaged me.

They'd always reacted instantly, mysteriously.

How come they always seemed so close, so accessible?

How come they never gave up on me, even when I challenged them?

Where did they get their wisdom, and how did they transfer it to me so easily?

Without warning, an astounding thought revealed itself with the impact of a land mine explosion. It was soundless. But the flash was so bright, so staggering, that it rocked my soul.

The bare truth was clear to me.

My 1,000 angels were never separate from me because they resided within me. They were *me* talking to *me*. They talked to me like my best self. They *were* my best self.

When I was being broken, I didn't have the insight to recognize myself in a survival mode. I glimpsed my angels through emotional cataracts formed by years and years of unshed tears layered one on top of the other. My vision was blurred. I was blinded by self-pity.

Every time I'd murmured sorry—sorry—sorry, I was attempting to console myself.

I felt sorry for me.

I had every right to wallow in my own despondency.

The obstacles placed in my journey were huge. I leaned on my excessively active imagination for solace. I see now that I, a needy girl, invented my shiny blob of 1,000 angels. They were born of my profound emotional needs.

Not only did they become real, they ruled my reality.

I needed them to teach me how to fathom my soul's capacity to withstand emotional pain, to outlast hardship, and how to become a durable, cohesive person. They were, and would always be, integral to my transformation

When the gut truth of me rose to the surface, I experienced an overwhelming feeling of serenity. The old chains of emotional abuse metamorphosed into smoke. I was free.

The angels, that wonderful glob image of them, had led me to gateway of healing I never knew existed. While they flitted to and fro, they were saving me from destruction either by others or to myself.

When I was forlorn, they found unique ways to entertain me.

They pulled me out of the dredges.

They found me great hiding places.

They talked to me in some passé angel language that I understood.

I loved my angels. I will always love them. I told them that.

Ah, yes, the angels were meandering around me now in a white steel circle that I invented. They eased me into my truth. They gave me a moment, a magic moment, to absorb the enormity of their grace.

"Everyone is born with a natural wisdom," are the

words I heard, "everyone on your planet has been given that gift. "

My head cleared. My soul cleared.

I wanted to know more about the power of emotional intelligence, how I could use it to my best advantage.

The angels perched on my inner ear.

"You think that what you bring to the real world seems inadequate, that you don't have important credentials?" they queried gently. "You think you can't compete with rivals better equipped educationally than you?"

I didn't answer.

The angels measured the uncertainty and self-doubt rattling within me.

"Can you release once and for all this whole burdensome lifetime load of accumulated abuse?" they asked.

I still didn't answer. I was all choked up, twitchy. It was hard for me to speak. I felt like a caterpillar squirming feverishly to get into butterfly mode.

My angels had more important things on their collective mind.

"Emotional intelligence is about motivation and empathy," I heard. 'It's about self-awareness. If you are emotionally intelligent, you become a leader. You are persuasive. When your confidence persists, when you don't let it lag, you can yield great influence on others. You are a born achiever."

The dumbbell? What about the dumbbell?

"You've exchanged emotional abuse for emotional intelligence," they said contentedly. "There is no dumbbell."

Their tone was congratulatory. This was huge. Being born happens only once in a lifetime, under duress. I was reborn as me, the real me, the emotionally intelligent me, free to start over.

I was happy.

Chapter Forty-Seven
Celebration

I found myself back at the ocean's edge. It beckoned me.

I jumped into the water, splashed in the waves, played like a child, and swam like a fish with the fish. My sorrows were as drowned as my trash.

This was the end of the dumbbell. This was the beginning of Sheila, the name my 1,000 angels had christened me long ago. Sheila reflected a golden glow, a luminescence that shone from the incredible knowledge that she'd never been dumb and that being female has a power of its own.

While I cavorted in the ocean, I envisioned myself standing straight, chin up and gaze steady, a self-possessed girl able to speak succinctly and logically, even when challenged by tough bosses or jealous counterparts.

I thought I could do this even when I felt like a fool.

I was dancing in the ocean with my soaking wet clothes on, even my shoes. Or maybe I was in my birthday suit. The angels never wanted me to feel weighted down. I must have looked foolish, playing in the waters as blissfully as an *au naturale* child.

This was my watery baptism. My 1,000 angels surfaced beside me.

They didn't drift. They walked on water, surrounding me with vapors that pacified me, welcomed me. They called the place where we were The Sea of Courage. They'd been trying to tell me all along that they were a part of me, that they existed in my soul, and that we spoke for and at each other.

Finally, at last, I understood that I was born with true grit. What my 1,000 angels did was bring that resoluteness to the surface of me, make it useable.

They told me to look at the horizon. It seemed to reach infinity.

"That's where you're going," I heard a voice rise from among the many splashes. The angels knew all creatives love discovery, fathoming the unknown, and, best of all, pushing peripheries.

My 1,000 angels told me from now on to listen for them, and to them, always with the labyrinth of my inner ear. "It does more than hear," the angels said while they romped in the sea. "It's what controls your balance." They would make sure that I was always balanced, and if I got woozy, they'd catch me before I fell.

"You're safe," they pealed as we splashed in and out of the waves merrily.

It was just the angels and me slipping and sliding on foam and bubbles.

Then we stood up and surfed without surfboards.

"You can do anything," is the muted and breathless prediction that seemed louder that the ocean's roar.

When the angels made that prophecy, I took to heart where it has always stayed.

Chapter Forty-Eight
The Man Upstairs

On a gloomy Monday morning, I was suddenly given orders to leave the smelly, sooty, and ink-stained stockroom to go, immediately, to the plush glassed-in office of the Commissioner. He was a highly decorated retired Army general who occupied the entire top floor of the opulent rococo State building.

This was a shocker. I'd been singled out. I'd been watched. My work life was about to take unforeseen twists and turns, charter the unknowns.

Despite all my brave trashing of negatives, "The Commish," as his underlings referred to the big boss, might be my firing squad, my condemner. I must have done something dreadfully wrong. Surely I was about to be fired. The trashed word, sorry, was edging its way into my consciousness.

I'd forgotten to trash the awful misgivings that sprung up whenever I was beckoned to come forward out of the shadows, make myself known, be seen, and speak up. I still feared the burn, any burn.

That fear nipped at me now.

A loose denim smock protected my sleeveless chemise. I shed the freshly laundered smock and hung it on a hook already stashed with a hump of smelly clothes. Mommy made my dress, and many just like it. She had an old portable Singer sewing machine that she pedaled with her feet. She'd collected a mish-mash of bargain fabrics plied from drastic sales.

The chemise, which remains a classic, became my uniform.

I always looked better than I felt heading for the stockroom, a foul place operated by the two disreputable men who smelled worse than their place of occupation.

The stockroom was not a place for high heels and red nails.

I wore both.

Provocative accessories were my only outward bluffs of bravado. Churning up inside me, ready to be unleashed, but not in the stockroom, were dreams of becoming a young achiever in the creative world.

I wore blinders, worked like a horse that wore blinders, and feigned that stockroom work was merely a circuitous path to becoming a recognized writer. My Daddy experiences taught me to keep my obsessions concealed or be punished.

Daddy's silence ruling had a positive side effect.

Competing creatives steal your ideas, your style, and your signature. It's better to keep yourself to yourself. And I did. I thought of this kind of silence as a form of protection.

Mommy noticed my straight face and my constant inward gaze of concentration. "You're always cooking up something. Too bad you never learned to play poker," she commented slyly.

She thought good card players were stealthy strategists who knew when to attack, when to block, when to make a move. Mommy didn't know that during all the years that I'd been stuck in silence, I'd been absorbing every nuance, every action, every meaning hidden in every word. I'd studied everything about every person who crossed my stage.

I didn't care about cards or any commercial games.

I cared only for writing dazzling stories, for implementing new ideas, for taking the ordinary and making it dramatic. I wanted to be a pioneer.

These were the breakthrough pulls hatching inside me.

Mommy's fine rags-to-riches look, my trusty stash of chemises, was based on her old and indelible ulterior motive. The potential Commercial Course job, for which I'd been demoted in high school, was always on her mind. If I looked good, I'd become a government clerk or, better, a secretary.

Daddy's influence wasn't dead. Mommy still wanted her dumbbell to become a clerk, an assistant to someone who sat on high. I never told her I wanted to sit on high OMO, which, by now, you know means "on my own."

Every day, before I left for the stockroom, she inspected me in one of her magnificent "sacks." That's what a chemise dress was called by Dior, a Paris haute couture legend of that era. He created a straight dress, devoid of any decoration, that slipped over the head like a long t-shirt, with or without sleeves.

"Sacks!" Christian Dior grunted to the international media who asked him to name his latest style. That one word, sack, was translated into international fashion headlines. Sacks were highly desirable.

Mommy, who always had hungry eyes for "the latest" copied Dior's lead.

The Paris look intrigued Mommy, who was proud to give me a Parisian look. She told me every day that I belonged in an office suite. "Thank you, Mommy," I said and visualized myself dressed as a professional journalist in a newspaper cubicle writing front-page stories.

Now I was in an elevator flying up to hierarchy territory

from the grubby downstairs, the lowest rung of the ladder. Doubt nagged me. I needed my hellish job below.

Now I was on high, in the Commissioner's presence. I'd been catapulted from the trenches into a great man's presence. He was more respectful than intimidating.

Newsletters told me that he was a retired, highly decorated hero who revered loyalty and people who had a knack for bull's eye precision. He ruled his bailiwick strictly, didn't tolerate laziness or losers, He ran his department with a focus on success or, as he called it, "victory." Everyone knew that. Even me.

Right now he was scrutinizing me as thoroughly as if he were still a formidable platoon commander on a critical inspection.

I stood straight and tall, at attention.

The two "pers" the angels taught me, perseverance and persistence, snapped into my thoughts. "That's what he expects of you," is what I heard bouncing off the white walls of this spectacular office with a view of the distant city skyline.

It was common knowledge that The Commish had been one of those exemplary generals who understood the complexities of being burrowed in a foxhole, expecting possible annihilation from an unseen enemy or even friendly fire.

I'd overhead office gossipers talking, even on elevators, that as nice as he seemed, he didn't tolerate fickle employee wars. He fired staff as easily as he had fired his old rifle.

The only war he fought now was to gain honor and recognition for the Department of Commerce, a place that he ran with military precision.

The Commish had a penchant for no-nonsense black leather furniture outlined with studs. He invited me to sit on the easy chair facing his fancy, highly polished mahogany desk. I passed muster.

Still, I steeled myself for the worst. Like Mommy facing a crisis, I folded my hands in my lap to appear calmer than I was.

Emotionally abused survivors have a bad habit that's hard to shake, much less trash. They automatically resist positivity because their experiences have usually ended in disappointment or disaster.

"Perseverance and persistence," I heard. I felt a nudge.

In my mind, I'd already started down the sorry—sorry—sorry track when the Commissioner, bald and bold, announced that he had a letter from Human Resources regarding me. Stiffened by fear that I held in check, I sat still.

He perused the letter. The gesture stoked my trepidation. I held my breath. Then, making eye contact with me, he spoke in baritone, disclosed that it was a letter of recommendation.

He never read it to me. He didn't offer to let me read it. He only summarized its contents.

The letter stipulated that I had done a good job, but I was too good for the stockroom. It indicated that I had a talent for using time effectively and showed a keen sense of responsibility. I'd never taken time off, even my vacation allotment. I had an exaggerated sense of duty.

Who wrote that golden letter? Had the angels prompted this recommendation? Had they worked their magic? I never knew.

The Commissioner was waiting for my response.

I hid myself in that old familiar place, silence. I said absolutely nothing. My expression didn't change. I froze. Perhaps it looked as if I was standing at attention—erect, upright and assertive.

The boss, who'd ruled in a crucible of war, leaned back in his black recliner, eyed me with a glint of admiration, and offered me the receptionist job on his floor, at a junior clerk salary.

My heart thumped.

But I remained unflinching. I was too traumatized to react. A sharp image of the antique key dropped directly in front of my eyes. The key! That's all I could see. The key! I stayed frozen, unblinking, staring at the key visible only to me. It was a very old amulet that opened doors that didn't fit the lock.

The key was magic. Forgiveness was magic. Being offered a new job was magic.

I woke up. I paid attention. I was alert.

"This involves a substantial raise and a small title," the Commissioner prompted. "Do you want the job?"

My 1,000 angels poked me.

"Yes, sir," I answered emphatically.

My anxiety had proven groundless. This was the culminating lesson in self-mastery. Finally, and fearlessly, I had to cancel the shadowy old dreads, acccpt that Daddy had been the Daddy of Distress, and that he was dead.

The Commissioner was the ruler of my future, my new commander in chief. I knew he was not a potentate. His eyes reflected kindness, plus the goodness of compassion.

That swift realization changed my mood, my outlook. It changed everything. I stood up, reached across the Commissioner's desk, and shook his hand. "Thank you, sir," I said with the eagerness of a child gifted with a new toy

"The new job starts tomorrow. Your desk is ready," the Commissioner said.

"Yes, sir," I repeated. My voice had a salutation in it, a sense of pride. This was my first step up from nothing.

The Commissioner smiled approvingly.

I was smiling too.

Chapter Forty-Nine
A Box of Bad

What inaugurated my new job was no smiling matter.

An authentic florist box, the rectangular size meant to hold long stem roses, sat enticingly in the middle of my new desk.

I looked for a gift card. There was none. The box seemed authentic.

It was fresh and clean. I was so distracted by the delightful notion of receiving flowers that I ignored the awkward twist of the second-hand red ribbon. It was tied clumsily.

My forgetfulness, later I would call it carelessness, boomeranged.

When I opened the box, snuggled in the crinkly tissue paper was a huge nasty cockroach. The gruesome black tormentor jumped toward me, swung like a pendulum, squeezed itself small, and vanished among my files.

This dirty trick oozed resentment and hostility. It was

disgusting. I quashed a scream. My hands shook like Mommy's. Someone jealous, someone in my immediate vicinity, hated me enough to put me in close touch with a filthy cockroach.

I knew a lot about venom and enmity within the family circle.

I didn't know that a person unknown to me, a stranger, could loathe me and terrorize me so shamelessly and without an obvious reason. The cockroach was a unique kind of burn. I was totally naïve about office wars. But all wars have a commonality: enmity. This was a sick trick. My superfluous knowledge of cockroaches is that they spread disease and multiply rapidly.

Only seconds had passed.

I plunked myself down at my new desk job with a modicum of forced efficiency.

Actually, I held onto the back of the desk chair and, somehow, willed myself to fall into it with as much poise as I could manage. I was living in cockroach land. I was living dangerously.

The cockroach was a revolting start to a new job.

I knew I had to appear as if everything was normal, had always been normal. I feigned phony stoicism. I mimicked Mommy sitting placidly while Daddy bullied her. I play-acted like Mommy had play-acted when Daddy attacked.

The telephone rang.

I was fooling myself and fooling the caller into thinking that the message I was taking for the Commissioner was the only thing on my mind.

My behavior, the way I conducted myself under the combined voodoo of a sudden cockroach and the startle of a sudden call, had been closely observed.

The department manager stood nearby, out of sight, and watched the nerve-wracking flight of the creepy pest fall into my surroundings. He'd seen me jolt and snap to attention. "This is perseverance," I heard anonymously from somewhere.

He took note.

I had answered the telephone amiably, as if there had been no cockroach incident. When I cradled the phone, the manager approached me and ordered, "Follow me."

Before we marched toward his office, he grabbed the flower box, tore it up, and disposed of it. A stranger had literally trashed my new trash! This was my primary lesson in human camaraderie, something foreign to me. My 1,000 angels must have earthly counterparts.

The man talked straight:

Look," he said frankly, "the telephone operator wanted to be the receptionist." He revealed this fact with an honesty and no-nonsense directness. "She still wants your job. She begged the Commish for it. She was turned down. She was furious, and she is still furious."

His frankness bowled me over.

"You were chosen impartially from a long list of candidates compiled by several department heads," he continued.

I'd never encountered anyone who spilled the god's honest truth without hesitation. I realized, too, that I'd earned this man's respect. I didn't know that I harbored that power. A fast whisper from oblivion whipped by me: "Respect yourself, and others respect you."

"Why me and not her? "I asked the question effortlessly. I had to understand the person, the motive, behind the cockroach gift.

His tone was both casual and penetrating.

"The Commish traced too many expensive personal calls to her switchboard, including some overseas, to Italy, to unknowns," the manager said frankly. "I saw her put the box on your desk. I didn't know what in it."

He paused. He underlined his point by speaking emphatically.

"What just happened disgraces her, not you," he said generously. "Remember that."

This man was my immediate boss, the person to whom

I reported daily.

He spoke like my angels, with integrity. He'd obviously lived his life on a high moral code.

"It's professional jealousy," he concluded, waiting for me to react.

I'd been mulling over straight shooters, how they make the best allies. They're trustworthy even when the chips are down. I must have seemed absent-minded. He expected an answer. When Mommy was at her lowest point, she was absent minded too.

Falling into silence when an answer was expected is a bad habit. It does not reflect emotional intelligence. I got a firm grip on myself.

"Do you understand the concept of professional jealousy?" he asked, connecting my job directly to the cockroach experience. "Can you move beyond it?"

Nothing was going to stop me. Not even a live cockroach living in my desk.

Yes, of course," I nodded.

My manager didn't know that I'd grown up in a house of combat. I'd learned about jealousy and bias and sexism and discriminatory competition at home. I did not want to be the loser on the job. I did not want to go from one war to another war.

I was sick of trash. My cockroach experience was trash. I trashed it.

That's how I found out that in order to survive, and succeed, you have to trash your trash immediately, all of it, or it weighs you down like a ball and chain.

A jealous female rival had served notice, a cockroach. Mommy had once handed me a potty of foul excrement from a baby's highchair. The messages were equally damning.

I'd emptied the potty in the toilet bowl, flushed it away.

Now I had to flush out a cockroach living in my immediate vicinity. A cockroach is a notorious hider. Maybe I'd never find it. Maybe it would never find me. I had to trash the *idea* of a cockroach around me. Someone I didn't know wanted to creep me out, destroy my potential on the job.

Doubts smacked me. But, this time, they were reasonable doubts.

What if the jealous switchboard operator didn't give me my calls? What if she refused to take messages if I was already on the telephone? What if I became the ineffective, incommunicado receptionist?

All my life, I'd burned in silence. I shook off Daddy's curse.

I was still in the manager's office. I spoke up for the first time. I said exactly what I thought. I used slang, my kind of slang. I equated a large cockroach, a fast producer, with being burned.

"Burn!" I exclaimed. "This could burn down my new job."

An emotionally abused girl, me, was trying out her wings for the first time.

The manager, a bearded man wearing a baggy old gray suit, either inherited or a thrift shop find, fiddled with his wrinkled plaid bow tie. It went crooked. He didn't straighten it. He just let my emotional "burn" outburst hang in the air between us.

I'd used a crooked word, burn, all my life, but only in angry conversations with myself.

"I want to prove to the Commissioner that I am worthy of his trust," I said.

I didn't tell this nice man who listened to his newest employee with remarkable tolerance, that my whole life I'd been starved of trust and confidence and honor and joy. I never mentioned that old shingled green house near the neighborhood market with its fishy smell. I didn't say that this job, this promotion, was my first escape route. I didn't say that I'd already dealt with cockroaches that weren't cockroaches.

The manager told me not to worry, that he'd have "a nice little talk" with the conspirator, explain to her that she was on thin ice. "I'll tell her she's being watched through a magnifying glass and that she'd better be an efficient worker...or else."

I liked the manager's "or else" implication. He'd witnessed a burn in progress. I also knew that promises, even half promises, could fly in the face of maliciousness. It was very difficult to believe in anything or anyone. I'd been burned too many times. But that day was the day I trusted a stranger.

That was the day I discovered somebody else, my manager, understood burn.

But not like I understood burn.

Chapter Fifty
Getting Over It

That night, when I tried to sleep, I was invaded by cockroach nightmares while wide-awake. I saw them crawling on the ceiling, on my bed, on the walls, everywhere. My 1,000 angels swooped onto my pillow. I heard them whisper they had "ridded" that pesky cockroach and, in fact, all abominable cockroaches in my general locale.

"Whoosh, they're gone," I heard, and I believed.

My angels didn't leave when I fell into a deep sleep. "Turn negatives around," they asserted while I played hopscotch in the heavens, jumped from star to star without fear of falling from the sky.

I awoke refreshed.

I'd been used to doing two jobs a day. I wrote lots of freelance stories and did piles of night school assignments within a regular work week. This receptionist's job was relatively lazy. There wasn't enough work to do. I felt a twinge of guilt. I was wasting valuable time. I didn't want the Commissioner, or my manager, to think that being immersed in semi-idleness suited me just fine.

I answered the phone politely.

I answered simple questions from visitors clearly and pleasantly.

I typed and filed official letters alphabetically, according to the letterhead. I directed or escorted guests to the offices of high-ranking executives. I became efficient in my duties. There was no cockroach contact.

Competency wasn't enough.

Something in me yearned to be more resourceful and innovative. I was a creative who was a greeter, someone who typed and filed. This was Mommy's dream job for me, going commercial. It was not my ultimate dream.

Release from the stockroom was a godsend. I thanked my lucky stars that I no longer worked in The Noise Room where the shadow of rape existed.

The angels reminded me of a prediction they'd made long ago. "Small successes can snowball," they chimed. "When you release your fears, all of them, you will release energies bubbling just beneath the surface of you."

It was a reminder to respect my potential and to acknowledge my untapped abilities. I worked in the Department of Commerce. Its purpose was to promote businesses that sold locally manufactured goods around the world.

A big fat manual, the department's official document, lay on my desk.

It explained the role and authority of the Department in undecipherable legislative language. Written by a team of high-priced lawyers, the legalese was impossible for an ordinary reader to grasp. It was official. It was boring. It was a huge waste of taxpayer dollars.

Remembering how I'd snuck into the legal section of the Widener, attempting to write a legal dossier, gave me an extraordinary idea that began as a whim.

In my spare time on the desk, without anyone noticing,

I completely rewrote that tedious legal document into plain English. It took a long time. I was meticulous to the point of being finicky. I rewrote what I wrote and then re-edited what I'd edited.

While I was doing what no one asked me to do, the Commissioner's focus on running his agency became conspicuously clear to me. His high position was centered on letting the world know that globally recognized products made in the state were seen everywhere—but who knew their origin?

I raided the files to which I was privy.

I found memos summarizing official government meetings. Company representatives from every region of the state had made sincere pledges to progress and to promote. Everything was still status quo.

I hunted for reports of new enterprises, new moves, new programs.

There were none. None!

An idea, imagined in its entirety, as if it were a done deal, triggered my imagination. I was afraid it would evaporate as rapidly as my 1,000 angels sometimes did. So I wrote down what I imagined, the bare bones of it, and then I wrote an expansion of the bare bones.

I hid my scribbles in my handbag. They were getting more and more substantial. Copycats abounded. In my journalism classes, I learned how easy it was for a competitive reporter to steal information. I had to protect my ideas from thieves. Saboteurs too. I'd learned about the rigors of sabotage at home, in the old days, when I was a dumbbell.

The idea bouncing in my imagination awakened my senses, held me in its thrall.

I thought about it morning, noon, and night. I dreamed it. I was like a girl possessed. That old Daddy oath of silence, once dreaded, came in handy.

My lips were sealed in protection of my scheme. I was the one-and-only person harboring this unique idea. It was so lucid, so coherent, that I thought of it selfishly, as "Sheila's Show."

Sheila was smart.

I was Sheila.

"Yes," I heard from somewhere and nowhere. "Yes, you're Sheila."

Chapter Fifty-One
The New World

If this weren't my moment, I would make it my moment.

I'd trashed years of condemnations. I was no longer subject to lifelong repercussions of Daddy's ongoing ostracism. Now I wanted commendations.

I was in an alternative place, emerging from the darkness of my past, standing front and center, in the light. The ultimate me was coming alive, waiting to prosper. I was frantic to create a professional life of my own.

Now I had actual tools.

Persistence and perseverance became my gadgets, my devices, and my utensils. This was formidable ammunition. I became far less passive. I had paid strict attention to my night class lectures. Assignments from a variety of editors demanded my being able to fulfill their different demands on deadline.

I had gained far more than the checks that were never mine. I had acquired a semblance of professional respect for myself. I was different. My differentness counted.

While I filed letters, I agonized over the "how" of presenting my idea.

When I answered the phone, I was mentally staging my project's complex components, meshing them into a delightful whole. In order to execute something unforgettable, I had to *picture* it fully executed in detail.

When I tossed and turned, unable to find peace of mind to fall asleep, I was mulling how to pick powerful key words to persuade the Commissioner succinctly that my idea was not only doable, it was irresistible. I was thinking of a small masterpiece, unique in execution.

I wanted him to see what I saw.

The angels fluttered around. They knew that indecision and insecurity had no place in the currency of my work life now. They knew all the secret unknowns of my soul. They urged me on. In my previous life, they'd spoken of taking a leap in faith.

This idea, it was a big idea, was that leap.

"Be yourself," they reminded me, and I knew I was talking to myself.

When I was a miserable child in the rickety green-shingled house, I thought the angels threw unreasonable standards at me. There were times when I thought they'd been unfair.

I had no inkling who I was or what lay ahead. They did. Their old refrain, "Be Yourself," made perfect sense now.

Together we had trashed my trash. I was not a lost soul anymore.

I was a *recovering* soul addicted to bullying and was now fighting to blossom into the real me. This was a new era. I had to adjust my self-image, push it into the radiance of uninterrupted positivity.

While I typed letters and more letters, I considered the dynamics of the word "*sell*." How could I present my proposal to the Commissioner flawlessly, my way, and be convincing? The idea had to be interpreted as a done deal, a fully executed package.

Salesmanship involves a certain amount of seduction and wooing.

That was not within the range of my abilities. I did not bewitch people. I was not a cunning con. I was the withdrawn dumbbell who hid in the shadows. Maybe the idea was too big, too enormous for a teenager to tackle. Maybe I'd bitten off more than I could chew.

"Just be you," is the thought that assaulted my senses.

Okay. Okay. Okay.

I'd have to present my project logically, explain it step by step. I had to be explicit. If the Commissioner had questions, I could leave no stone unturned. If I got into his office, if I stood before him with an idea, I had to be prepared to give him the right answers to whatever question he threw at me. I had to do this without hesitation.

Again and again, I heard the words, the key words, "persistence" and "perseverance" whispered into my once pretend-deaf ears.

Persistence means moving ahead despite opposition.

Perseverance means being steadfast, tenacious, when facing difficulty or delay.

They're both about keeping your eye on the ball. They're almost twin words with one connection: focus.

I had to be very, very focused.

I prepared a formal dossier, a detailed record of how this project could be accomplished. If Daddy had let me go to college the regular way, this might have been the making of a thesis. But I did write the semblance of a thesis once, at the Widener.

Obnoxious memories of vicious putdowns still cropped up now and then. I knew that bad flashbacks have to be squashed or they would take over.

I reminded myself that self-control was the pivot on which emotional intelligence revolves.

If I got an appointment with the Commissioner, I knew I'd be allotted a small amount of measured time. I did not want to hesitate or hold back. I did not want to appear meek. Salespersons are naturally gregarious and cleverly insistent. I'd been emotionally disabled.

"That's not true" is the murmur I heard from nowhere. It was barely audible but it came at me with such force that all my negative second thoughts vanished.

I re-evaluated my contemporary self, my pluses.

I was organized to a fault.

I made thorough notes, just like I'd done on my Widener fling, just like I'd done in my countless freelance work.

Even when severely fatigued, twisted, I forced myself back to alignment.

When I balanced myself, I was steadier and sharper and smarter. I tried to stay in that orbit. The angels helped me. They told me good things about myself.

I was a reliable producer, someone with a one-track mind who was totally immersed in the assignment at hand.

I took risks that panned out.

I could read between the lines.

I had assimilated the rudiments of emotional intelligence, maybe more.

I began to accept that while I lived through years of abuse, I was being honed for better things. Then doubts assaulted my new-found confidence. Maybe the idea was too big, too enormous for a teenager to tackle. Maybe I'd bitten off more than I could chew.

On the other hand, I'd crashed into enormous walls of resistance for years and lived to tell the tale.

That was the point. I'd been in combat. I knew the stuff of opposition intimately. I'd been readying all these years to tackle what I now thought of as "something big."

Chapter Fifty-Two
Going For It

My project idea was two-sided.

It was both absurdly simple and extremely complicated.

The simple part was wanting to write, produce, and commentate a musical fashion show featuring everything chic—clothes, shoes, handbags, jewelry, hats, and all kinds of accessories—made in local factories within the state and distributed around the world.

The Commissioner's state was home to hundreds of manufacturers of anything and everything fashion, from furs to sneakers. The show would be christened "The State of Fashion."

The complicated part was, indeed, complicated.

I would have to cull the many products and acquire the many models, musicians, and performers needed to produce a coordinated show, to say nothing of a staging space, live music, a carpeted runway, and spotlights everywhere.

I knew I'd have to break the project down into separate

pieces and reassemble them into a cohesive whole. Despite its immensity, I imagined the project as complete, finished. I saw it in motion, the models on the runway, the music, the lights, and even my spoken commentary.

These clear visions came to me while I spent hours at the filing cabinets. At night, in my dreams, I envisioned the finished show. It was alluring. It had to be.

Still, I had shillyshally moments. I had no track record. I was only a receptionist. After all it was just me, the girl dumbbell, basking in what was little more than figments of my impossibly wild imagination.

The angels reminded me what I already knew. I was an old soul.

I'd already lived a lifetime of fiery emotional experiences compressed into a small amount of time.

That was no longer the total barometer of me.

The words "perseverance and persistence" often rang softly inside me. Those two key words, stuck to my soul with some sort of immovable glue. Sometimes I thought of them as my trusty silver bells.

Now was the time to get rid of every speck of what Mommy facetiously called, "things that ail you." She never gave feces its slang name, even when she pushed that dirty potty under my nose. Merde had no place in my life.

I had to get real, articulate my dream scene into a real scene. I had to convince the Commissioner to let me knock on doors that had been overlooked. "Just be you," the angels sang over and over.

Their positivity became my positivity.

I asked for an appointment with the Commissioner.

He heard me out.

"Fine," he said, "but only if you continue to do the receptionist job well, and it doesn't cost the Department a penny."

He had drawn explicit red lines in the sand. The words were written in neon.

I hesitated.

"Persistence" rang inside me. It wasn't loud enough. I had doubts.

Maybe I'd already encountered barriers too big to handle. I'd been stopped in my tracks. "Not a penny," the Commissioner repeated.

"Perseverance" swished through my core.

The idea of obstacles flashed at me just like the red flashers on the truck that stole my doggie. I stopped in my tracks. The Commissioner sensed my fumble.

He studied me with one sharp cursory glance.

Almost as an afterthought, he quickly nodded and said gently: "But I think you're on to something."

The complexities of my project had just become significantly larger. I'd have to do two jobs simultaneously. I had no budget. All I had was a "yes" with strict boundaries.

My silence, my old and natural hiding place, gobbled me up. I'd been a fool to think I could pull off a project that way, way bigger than me.

I became speechless.

The angels were somewhere close. I heard them hum, in a harmonious chorus that now was the time for me to surf without a surfboard.

But I still couldn't find my voice.

The Commissioner started to ask if I thought I could really pull this off, if I could execute this project with confidence and sophistication.

Before he changed his mind, I said emphatically, "Yes, Sir," and headed toward the door. "We're onto something splendid," I added over my shoulder.

The Commissioner didn't know that I'd worked two jobs and gone to college at night and washed dishes and cleaned bathrooms and scrubbed floors at home. He didn't know how good my job-juggling skills were.

I'd been trained by destiny, and by the 1,000 angels, to tackle all kinds of unreasonable issues simultaneously. I had impeccable orientation. I'd learned the hard way about coping with obstructionists. These positive characteristics were embedded in what remained of my sorry—sorry—sorry personality.

I thought of Lucille.

I promised myself that I'd never say sorry—sorry—sorry again unless it was a legitimate apology. Now was time to put my courage to work *at* work, to turn my life around.

I heard the angels humming a song of approval. They'd snitched a line from "I Believe," one of Mommy's favorite songs. When I was little, she played the piano, and we sang together happily: "I believe for every drop of rain that falls, a flower grows…"

Or was that me humming to myself?

Chapter Fifty-Two
Doing It Right

A flop was out of the question.

No haywires for me.

This idea was good, but it was also a mad gamble, full of risks. Unexpected or unintentional blunders, errors, slip-ups, misjudgments, or gaffes could snowball into a professional disaster.

My beginning could be my end.

If I goofed, I'd have to figure out how to fix things. Better that I make good decisions, take precautions. My time had come. I'd always wanted to establish new frontiers, make them my own. I had to make this project shine.

My beginning had to be a wonderful beginning.

The Commissioner had staked enormous confidence in me. I wanted to make him proud the way I would have made a good Daddy proud. I had to be worthy of the leeway he'd given me.

I composed myself. I spent my energies carefully. I was

the architect of my project, its orchestrator. I needed to have all the facts at hand in one place. I wrote everything down logically, meticulously, in excruciating detail, knowing that, in the end, I could tie all the loose ends together nicely.

My notes were the backbone of my renaissance. I took them home. I slept with them. I played, sometimes overplayed, my ideas until there was no more room for more scribbles. I wrote more than one addenda. If I wanted my ideas to turn out fine, I'd have to fine tune them. I was always polishing my ideas until they shined.

The newspaper editors who'd hired me in the recent past noticed my sudden absence from the freelance scene. When they found out what I was doing, they'd be my critics. Unique shows like this had never been done before under government auspices. Uniqueness was the essence of important news coverage. Interested newspapers started asking questions, lots of questions.

I summed up the project in a press release on the Commissioner's stationery. He initialed his approval.

I was good to go.

What I wanted, after the first press release, were eye-catching feature stories with bold headlines bolstered by amazing photos. If the show glittered and gleamed enough to inspire the press covering the event, headlines would explode.

Journalism is a language of words. Eye-catching visuals dramatize the story. When pieced together well, they become dynamite.

Then I went on a "hunt."

I used my work telephone discreetly.

When incoming departmental calls lapsed, I picked up the receiver and went on a selling spree.

On a late Friday afternoon, a taxi whisked me to an assembly of excited wannabe models at a local modeling school. I was upfront with the Director. This was to be a public service. The models wouldn't be paid.

"List our school on your program," he said. "List the

models' names and their communities. Do that, and the students will accept no monetary compensation."

He beamed: "We'd be honored too."

I chose the prettiest, skinniest, tallest, and most confident girls from a large group of contestants. The meeting was a cross between an audition and a social gathering. There was a lot of giggling and chattering. The gist was that I was young, just like them, and running the show.

This turned into an asset.

From all the careless chitchat, I learned that retail fashion directors were usually pompous old ladies who had unbendable rules. My youth was a bonding tool. I was not set in my ways. I spoke a few opening words. I described myself as a creative who controlled without being a control freak. I got applause mixed with appreciative chuckles.

I heard a semblance of esteem.

I know all about the sting of rejection. I used discretion when I made my choices. The Director lined up the contestants who paraded past me one by one. The prospective models carried number cards, no names.

When the models left, I gave the director the winning "numbers." When I left, he posted their names on a bulletin board.

Men offer a handshake, and it's an honorable binding agreement.

The Director and I shook hands. A contract was made. That clasping gesture gave me equal footing. I felt as if I were on a high, like when the angels hurtled through the forest and dangled on the moon.

But I was also savvy enough to acknowledge that this friendly agreement had to be confirmed on official departmental letterhead, signed by the Commissioner. "It's good that you're being cautious," he said admiringly.

The Commissioner also issued another order: he told me he needed a legal form drawn up, signed by him and each company involved, to make sure that the work I was doing was, as he put it, "in accordance with every law on the books."

I had that signed protection in my possession within a week, the very week that I was shopping around for a suitable location.

The show's address had to be an important downtown hotel with a lavish function room. I telephoned the general manager of the best hotel in the city. I stated my case.

"Of course, you can have the best public room if it is booked now." His businesslike reference to "booking" made my heart sink. Without a showplace, there was no show.

"How much?" I asked efficiently.

I was quaking in my boots.

"If you credit us on your program, it's free," he replied matter-of-factly.

For a moment, I felt like the angels who made snowballs out of surf. I had him sign the legal form. When he did, his company's lawyer was present. I was learning how to follow protocol, how to avoid criticism, legal penalties, or any repercussions that suggested trouble.

I was learning firsthand that everything is business, including my governmental offshoot of show business, had to follow the rules. There were not like Daddy rules. They were rules I understood and respected, rules by which I was being given a way to express myself out loud, in public, in front of an audience.

The Commissioner, watching my strength gain momentum, had further detailed legal insurance papers be drawn up to cover all possible losses, including accidents and injuries. I sat in on these legal meetings in his office, as a silent observer.

I learned, learned, learned like a college intern learns.

When I wasn't doing my receptionist job, I was off to find a model who was a singer who could dance. The head of a prestigious music school in the city had just such a triple-talented senior who was on her way to Juilliard.

"She'll work with you, no salary, if you mention her

and our school," he offered. "We're involved in her scholarship funding. She wants to pay us back."

I felt as if the angels had plucked stars out of the heavens and hid them under my pillow. I made sure all signed and countersigned legal forms went to the Commissioner's lawyers.

I kept all my papers in order.

I never left them in the office.

I still took them home every night.

When I slept, they always slept with me.

A pianist. I needed a great pianist who could segue from classical to modern. The piano had to be a finely tuned grand piano. I wanted a white piano, Liberace style.

I also needed seasoned union men to handle the moving spotlights.

And gold chairs with red velvet seats. The guests had to feel like royalty. The sturdy runway had to be thickly carpeted, look opulent, with everyone's eyes riveted on the models' exaggerated slinks. They would be strutting in everything manufactured within the State. Perfection. That's what I wanted.

Most of all I needed workers to do the actual set-up.

I called the hotel manager back. Monsieur Pierre was originally from France.

In tranquil business tones, as if I'd been born to do the improbable, I asked him for the world. "*Oui*," he said. "*We have everything and everyone available on the premises.*"

Even the requested pianist was on his payroll, and he'd make him available. All his workers were members of unions. They'd be paid according to that standard. "No worries about strong men to do the heavy work," he chuckled while signing all the legal papers I handed over.

He made another hospitable suggestion, very French, very much in keeping with the *l'heure bleue*, Paris's twilight hour, when everyone's thoughts turn from tea to wine and roses.

He went a giant step further. "How about a brief

reception after the show, chilled chardonnay, and hors d'oeuvres, to be served by tuxedoed waiters?" He added an incentive to fill in my silence, "We'll keep the music going."

He was talking big, big money. He saw the reluctance in my glance. "I have no budget," I said coolly.

"*Rien*," he replied. I heard "never mind."

Question marks were scrolled in my eyes. He read them.

"You didn't ask," the manager assured me. "I am making the offer."

Yes! Oh, yes! I felt like the angels who plucked stars from the sky.

I told him I'd have the models pirouette among the post-show audience who could inspect close-up what they'd seen at a distance. This was a new twist, something unexpected.

When I smiled, delighted, thinking this was a glorious gift, he spelled out his strategy. This was a lucrative business deal. Period.

"Your audience is our future clientele," he said. "We want them to think of our Hotel as a future destination."

I felt like the 1,000 angels who navigated oceans without getting wet.

The invitations? Fine watermarked paper. I also needed envelopes and response cards. Money, money, money. Programs and invitations had to be color coordinated. Blue on white. The colors of the State flag. Money, more money.

I called the most expensive printer in the area, the one who catered to the city's elitists, the literati, the politically famous, and especially dynasty debutantes and brides.

"What are the figures?" the printer asked.

I knew he meant how much do I want to spend? I deflected his question. I gave him a rough estimate of how many invitations I planned to send. "I need 750 invitations," I said knowing that I had no expenditure.

I figured maybe seventy-five people would come. Only ten per cent of invitees reply "yes." I'd learned that in a nighttime college course. I was playing, poker, Mommy's metaphor for negotiating, for outsmarting someone.

"Put us on your program," he said. "That's our price."

The Commissioner's legal forms confirmed the deal.

When the agreement papers were signed, sealed and delivered, I felt like my 1,000 angels who'd hurdled through a dark forest and dangled from the trees without a hitch.

Dignitaries, like the governor's wife and spouses of the city's leading politicians and aristocrats, headed the invitation list. It would be primarily a media show. But the local celebrities in the audience would delight the columnists and reporters who doted on name-dropping.

The day before the show, the local television outlet for a national network telephoned to say it was sending a cameraman. "It's going to be on the 6:00 o'clock evening news," he announced in a hurried telephone call.

The impetus was speeding up, taking shape.

The psychology behind the show was to demonstrate to the press that my Commissioner was in perfect tandem with some of the internationally known fashion firms within his geographical jurisdiction. The Commissioner's subliminal message, "we're promoting our own," would be presented in the form of cutting edge theater, a contemporary fashion show set to music.

How often is the obvious overlooked? When I couldn't find something in the kitchen, Mommy used to laugh and say: "That's because it's sitting in front of you."

I felt as if a door had been unlatched, as if a bolt had popped open inside me, as if my crushed creative impulses had been unsealed.

Fashion manufacturers across the state opened their showrooms, opened their locked collection closets, even on Sundays.

I picked through a million racks and culled items that I thought would capture the headline. I fitted the models on the premises. Mirror reflections, unavoidable, made one model blurt: "You should model."

I looked at her as if she'd lost her mind. But she'd seen what I didn't see. I was beginning to look like Mommy.

I pulled together a special collection of clothes-costume jewelry-handbags-shoes-hats as if I was an experienced Vogue magazine editor. I knew who should wear what. I can't explain how I knew. I listened to my instinct. I chose fashions that pleased the eye. I knew what the photographers wanted to shoot, overstated glamour.

The chosen clothes, in plastic covers, hung on covered racks on wheels. They were insured and trucked to a locked space in the hotel, the one that kept on giving me privileges.

The Commissioner asked to see all the signed legal papers.

They were in good order.

When the invitations came, I'd addressed them by hand on a Sunday sitting at my desk in an empty office. I worried about the postage costs.

The Commissioner eyed the elegant custom watermarked stationery and the prestigious list of invitees. He said okay on the stamps. He never treated me as a teenager. In his eyes, I was a young woman on a roll. He asked for a detailed updated written report on my progress.

When he read it, he gave me a key to the office so I could use the telephone and the typewriter at any time, seven days a week.

And I did.

Daddy had broken my heart by not letting me use my legs to ride a bike or use my skates. He broke my legs when he excluded me from walking to the nearby field where my high school football team made the regionals. He broke my legs again by not letting me move around, be a normal girl. He had me in a sort of straitjacket that prevented me from taking a step forward.

This time I broke a leg in the show business sense. The former stockroom girl, now the receptionist, was in the process of pulling off a major coup for the Commissioner and his Department.

Chapter Fifty-Three
The Game

It was show time.

When the high voltage lights studding the long runway were flicked on, the jam-packed audience registered a clamorous buzz.

My hearing was on high frequency too.

Loud exclamations exploded from a roomful of anxious strangers waiting for me, the dumbbell, to deliver the goods. My fantasy had become real.

Stage fright burst into a tug-of-war with my confidence. The butterfly that had landed on my nose much, much earlier in my snagged journey, was now fluttering in my stomach.

I remembered Lucille again. Our musical evening. Most of all I remembered the indelible image of that genius orchestra maestro with his magical baton

I had a baton. I was about to direct my own ensemble. I, the dumbbell, was about to prove that dumbbells can rise from any stampede.

I felt queasy. This was a crucial turning point. I was rising. I walked to the dais, a high place. I'd been in high places before. But not literally.

Posthaste, facing the first big signpost of the rest of my life, I envisioned my new reality. I had a voice and a microphone that defied silence. I had a commentary I'd built from far-flung words scrambled into something coherent, something potentially fascinating.

I took my usual three deep yoga breaths.

"Drop dumbbell from your vocabulary," someone said from somewhere. "Remember perseverance and persistence."

The cautionary tale slipped effortlessly into my ear. I threw caution to the winds. Yes, yes. Quickly, more quickly than I thought possible, I got ahold of myself. Or was I assisted? The angels then dropped the word, gallant on me. "Be gallant."

Long ago I'd looked that word up in my school dictionary. It meant brave. I had to be brave. I took a sweeping glance at the scene I'd painted, not with brushes, but with grit and gumption. The emotional abuse I'd borne at home, all those terrible years, had developed my stamina, my endurance.

I crossed my fingers, thanked my angels and stood ramrod straight.

When I launched that show, I launched myself.

Hordes of almost-tardy newspaper and wire service photographers, militant men who snubbed ties and favored jeans, had elbowed their way into this elegant ballroom hampered by what they lugged: clumsy tripods and heavy cameras in dirty canvas bags.

They jostled for space. They were squished.

Tough media rivals in close quarters are not above a brawl. I was glad that I'd asked for on-site security. I'd thought uniformed men standing at attention might be a nice touch. Now I realized that they were essentials.

I was in serious learning mode.

Later, in dreamy recapitulation, I realized that the sum of all my impressions—from my first meeting with the Commissioner to this place onstage --is what self-taught means. Unschooled, untutored information acquired on one's own leads to independence. I was free of Daddy. I was free to think for myself. I was an independent.

Sounds of Disney movie music, the opening song, wafted toward me. "When You Wish Upon a Star."

What? What? I was on a first name basis with esoteric angels who played among the stars, angels who'd invited me to join them. The angels who put "star" in my vocabulary were dancing around the footlights and...

Click-click-click. Whirr, whirr.

When the show was in full swing, the photographers stared their lens on models who gyrated and spun on exaggerated high heel stiletto shoes that were like miniature stilts. The models weren't just living for the moment. They were living in the moment.

Photographers also shot VIP's seated on those lush red velvet cushion chairs, perusing my fashion show program, a double spread page.

Down the program middle I'd roped a narrow, fringed, bright blue ribbon that emulated a *book*mark. It was a secret salute to my Widener escapade. Officially I told the Commissioner that the blue was the same shade as the State flag. His lips curled into an approving smile.

During a round of applause, deafening, I tried to locate Mommy in the audience. She was there, somewhere, and...

"Keep your eyes peeled on the models" I heard. "No distractions."

The Twiggy-types, all young amateurs who assumed an exaggerated skinny-as-a-twig look, projected a sophistication usually not associated with teenagers. They twirled and whirled like the professional models they were not.

Early on, I'd decided that my "girls," that's how I referenced my chic peers, would all wear identical wigs in primary colors straight from my paint box. The "no-hairspray" wigs were coiffured identically: straight bangs dipping into straight chin-length pageboys that moved.

When a Twiggy, any Twiggy, either sensed or saw a photographer's focus fastened on her, there was instant runway action. She bobbed her pretty head. Her mobile Sassoon–inspired coiffure swung around to caress her face. She flirted overtly with glinty eyes and an alluring body stance.

A popular pre-Feminist phrase then was "a woman's best accessory is a man."

The models were actresses who did what comes naturally. Each had her own coquette tease. But the focal point was always the same. Each click-click and whir-whir of the cameras represented a make-believe man of special interest.

One model, representing them all, had asked me if I'd permit a looser, more contemporary kind of modeling.

"Show me," I'd fussed during a rehearsal.

The spokesperson model parodied the strict classic model swagger that was reigning at Paris' Coco Chanel and Yves Saint Laurent salons. It was a strict and stiff. Only the feet minced. Paris models, who never seemed to blink, looked like make-believe department store mannequins whose only human trait were their feet.

Then, in sharp contrast, the model went modern.

She swayed, sashayed down the runway. It was contemporary and exuberant. She looked like a woman of purpose, someone planning to get things done. And she smiled when she twirled and swirled.

I said yes, yes, yes.

Some of the models and musicians in the real show got so pumped by the palpable audience enthusiasm that they forgot that I'd established boundaries. They improvised scenes, some dangerous, that didn't work in practice sessions. They forgot that I'd declined dangerous ploys. The angels, they were there, must have kept the ambulances at bay.

One sexy model, a jazz singer, flung open her arms to the audience, wiggled her fingers and derriere, strutted and danced recklessly down the runway while enunciating the phrasing of her songs like a Broadway star.

The still cameras clicked madly. The television cameras whirred madly.

Applause-applause. It got so loud that no one could hear my commentary. I had to stop.

Then came two other wonderfully executed astounding ad-libs

The male pianist scrambled onto the closed lid of the grand piano and played the notes lying on his stomach, arms outstretched, fingers on the keys. Mozart is said to have pranked his audience this way too. The impromptu act had failed in rehearsal. Unbeknownst to me, the pianist had practiced and practiced until he got it right.

In quick succession, there was a palpable astonishment, then a silence born of surprise and, finally, delighted laughter and an ovation.

The pianist brought the house down.

The next model, a female dancer who'd performed the choreographed ragtime segment, kicked high and fell into a successful split on the narrow runway.

She'd failed during the final rehearsal. We'd eliminated the chancy split.

But, without telling me, she too, had practiced and practiced. When the crucial show time moment came, her split was perfect. Another deserved ovation.

My three adventurers re-emphasized what the angels had insisted: I could inspire people to do impossible things I'd never worked with a team. I'd never had collaborators. It was the first time I'd seen people, relative strangers, take dramatic chances under my aegis. It was the first time I'd taken a chance on myself.

It was all very, very good.

I'd written the post-show commentary, centering on the

Commissioner and the specialness of his focus. Our local manufacturers were nationally known unknowns. What the public wasn't aware of is that some of the greatest fashion products used by global couturiers were manufactured in our state. The Commissioner had a question for everyone: did you know?

When I said that, applause erupted.

Reporters took copious notes just like I did as a fledgling freelancer.

I had tucked the ancient forgiveness key in my purse for good luck. I'd put it under the podium. I'd made sure it touched my toes. True to its legend, it seemed to open closed doors that I never thought were accessible. At the close of the show, while the audience delivered a standing ovation, my 1,000 angels whispered that this launch represented the rest of my life.

It was raining bouquets,

"The State of Fashion" made splashy headlines in all the major city and regional newspapers. The wire services picked up either the story or the photos, sometimes both. Every city or town that boasted a model, a fashion, anything or anybody local, carried the story.

The publicity skyrocketed.

An avalanche of excellent reviews hit the Commissioner's desk. He didn't attend. At the last minute, he got cold feet. The weapons that I was using were not his kind of weapons. They were unfamiliar to him. Perhaps he was afraid that he'd had given me too much liberty.

Instead his wife, his representative, attended as Mrs. Commissioner. She asked Mommy to sit with her group. The angels reminded me, in a hushed tone, that they'd predicted that someday I'd be Mommy's salvation.

This was that moment.

"You've proven yourself," Mommy said later. She was proud.

Mrs. Commissioner, with Mommy in tow, was invited to sit with the Governor's wife. The important ladies liked

Mommy. Her beauty had matured without noticeable diminishment. She was charming, intelligent, informed. Mommy fit in perfectly with the aristocratic ladies. She was born to this elite class. But her hands shook.

The Commissioner got the show's verdict immediately from both his wife and the governor's wife, true friends since their college days.

They told him that he'd achieved something spectacular for his Department and the State. The show portrayed him as a great visionary, an executive with a razor-sharp awareness of how his state's famous manufacturers, hidden in far-flung rural places, could be illuminated and honored.

The Commissioner was lauded far and wide by the press as someone with the foresight to put State-made fashions on an elegant stage so that the public could see what they'd never seen before.

For him, it was about pride of State.

For me, it was about pride of me.

Chapter Fifty-Four
An Office

The next day I was called into Commissioner's office.

He closed the door. This was a private conversation.

He asked me if I could make this an annual event. He offered me my own cubbyhole. There would be Ivy League college interns to help me next time.

The switchboard operator, who never crossed me again with a cockroach or any other stunt, was given my receptionist job, temporarily, on a six months probation period. There had been office chitchat about my hiding a cockroach in the top drawer of her desk.

I've always disapproved of revenge. Everyone deserves a second chance.

Besides, she'd contributed substantially to the show.

I'd given her the crucial lineup of the models' entrances and exits on time. It was her job to handle the model's comings and goings to coincide with my commentary. I put her in charge backstage. I made her my partner. This was a test of her vigilance, her efficiency, and her loyalty.

Our department manager told her this was her big chance to rectify her cockroach trick. She came through with flying colors. After the show, amid all the backstage confusion, she told me she'd found and killed the cockroach. "I'm sorry," she said and meant it. I knew all about sorry—sorry—sorry.

A national trade newspaper chain headquartered in New York City had a bustling regional Bureau near my office. The Bureau Chief saw the publicity, tracked me down, and offered me a staff writer's job.

It paid twice my government salary. I didn't have to freelance anymore. I would be a real writer with a full-time writing job. I was reluctant to say goodbye to the Commissioner. I'd forgotten that I knew how to cry. When Daddy was on the attack, I kept it all in, bundled it all up. It was the only time I cried in public.

The New York editor of that national news organization assigned me to write a piece on affluent Radcliffe girls who were unwittingly starting a national trend with their long straight swinging hair.

A New York fashion photographer was flown in to partner me. Together we roamed Radcliffe land, hunting down students with long hair that fluctuated in the breeze like ocean waves and, thanks to impeccable cuts, fell into place without looking mussed.

He had a zoom lens. He could do remarkable close-ups. I told him when to shoot.

The "Cliffies," that's what ordinary people called the crème de la crème Radcliffe students who didn't suspect they were being photographed. They dashed here and there, hair fluttering-flipping-soaring to and fro. The improvisational photos caught perfectly the sassy mood of flying coiffures.

I wrote a tongue-in-cheek story, pointing out that you could tell the freshmen from the seniors by the length of their hair.

I credited a mastermind orphan, Vidal Sassoon, a poor Londoner, who'd leapt from doing shampoos to achieving a net worth of $200 million as the world's hairstyle king

Sassoon not only freed girls from rollers and excessive hairspray, he was paid a whopping $5,000 to chop off actress Mia Farrow's long hair for a '60s movie. "Rosemary's Baby."

I made a facetious fashion forecast.

High school graduates heading for Radcliffe, and other colleges, were begging for pricey Vidal Sassoon gift certificates instead of cars.

Girls everywhere imagined themselves looking like the swinging Radcliffe girls.

The trend exploded into a revolution.

That giddy story was my lucky story.

Chapter Fifty-Five
Good Luck

I was busy on the telephone wrapping up an interview, writing on deadline. The editor of one of America's ten top newspapers was on another phone. Leave a name and number, please. There was no time to take the call then or even to return it promptly.

My favorite night school professor, the one who started the freelance me, had hammered home a rule to avoid any kind of distraction that leads to mistakes. "Concentrate on the job at hand," he'd warned. "That's how stories get sloppy." The chief editor on this job put it another way, via a sign attached to his door. "No boo-boos allowed here," it warned.

My colleagues griped about the pressure. I doted on it.

I'd grown up in the house of pressure, the bad kind. The job pressure felt wonderful. It challenged me to be a much better writer than I thought I was. I had a legitimate by-line.

My stories got good play. I was not Daddy's putty girl. I was a young woman in transition. I was Sheila, not "She."

The big-time newspaper editor called me again the next day.

I hesitated before taking the call. I had never completely conquered my Daddy paranoia. Every now and then I'd fall into the old pattern of thinking someone wanted to use me either to gather hard-to-get information or to criticize my work.

I was a professional now, not a Dumbbell.

I took the call

A symphony of words. I heard my epiphany.

The managing editor of the famous newspaper wanted to interview me for the coveted Fashion Editor job. That job paid double my current salary, and there were stock options. Two hundred applicants from across the country had already been interviewed. They were eyeing me. They hired me.

"We found her in our back yard," the publisher jabbered to the press and other notables attending a lavish cocktail party in my honor. His ad-lib, a throwaway line, was dotted with an ethereal twist of irony.

The hotel function room had a huge oyster shell backing the podium at which he stood. It was eerily similar to the stage setting of that musical evening with Lucille, the night she assured me I was born creative. Somehow the two shells linked the old me to the new me. That shell was an uncanny symbol.

Even the publisher's "back yard" reference pinpointed my past.

It was in my back yard, long ago, where my doggie was kidnapped.

It was in my back yard, long ago, that Daddy gave Mommy pearls that weren't graduated, and that ruckus influenced how I graduated.

It was in my back yard, long ago, that I got an awful premonition that I'd be pulled out of high school before graduation.

It was from my backyard, long ago, that my glob of 1,000 angels walked through barriers and drifted toward me, arms outstretched, chanting wisdoms that egged me on.

I was in a different cave on high now. It had footlights. It involved a writing life on the international scene. Mrs. FDR's prediction, "if you can write you can do anything," was a done deal. Just like the angels foretold, things had turned around. I'd climbed to the other side.

My new editor, who liked red bow ties and socks to match, wanted his fashion pages to go global immediately. "You're the kid to do it," he'd said approvingly.

"Kid" was a term of endearment. My editor rarely used my name. He knew nothing about Daddy's curses, the dumbbell word, or me as "She."

He was picking me up, goading me to run fast, get ahead of my competitors. He trusted me enough to put his newest dream for his newspaper in my hands. He wanted fashion stories that had a global twist. He had faith in my ability. He knew that although I was a kid in years, I was born an old soul.

I know for sure that was the exact moment that all my burn, the incessant singe, and sizzle, became harnessed energy. I had become the emotionally intelligent person my glob of angels foretold.

Chapter Fifty-Six
More Good Luck

In the '60s, newspapering was a male bastion. Few women landed significant writing jobs in the print world. Covering women's interests, especially fashion, was a big honor then. Within a month, I hopped from Paris to Rome, from London to Madrid, and from Dublin to Athens.

My assignment was to cover the haute couture shows.

My editor called me into his corner office for a goodbye and good luck meeting. He spoke with such simple eloquence that I thought the 1,000 angels had nudged him too.

"Kid," he said as I sat facing him in a banged-up garage sale rocking chair, "call the shots as you see them." His crossed feet were perched on his desk and in my face. I didn't care. "Don't just report," he said. "Assess."

Staring at a man's shoes with holey soles was not the kind of male putdown that intimidated me. I never joined the first Feminists who were loud-mouthed lionesses. Daddy had pushed me around, made me silent and passive. Now my new boss, my commanding officer, was advising me to speak out loud, to make my stories bold. I was the feminist who never became a Feminist.

"Oh, yes," I replied, thinking about Daddy's ancient key. "And thank you for opening this new door."

Then he did the oddest thing.

While his feet remained on his desk, he saluted me.

The salute, a symbolic gesture, had great magnetism. It liberated me. I felt the joy and emotional sustenance of simple respect, something Daddy never thought a woman deserved. That's how I came to be like no other fashion editor of my era.

I did not write reverently about the absurdly perfect clothes in the $10,000-$100,000 range, beautiful clothes outside the financial orbit of most women.

I was not a worshipper at the altar of fashion designers who were as famous as movie stars.

My newspaper had plunked me down in some sort of weird fairytale land, and the best I could do was to interpret the meaning behind this amusing and amazing and absurd make-believe.

When I saw malnourished mannequins traipse down the runway in sheer see-through blouses worn over nothing, I wrote that the designer's message was that women should be free from ties that bind, bras included.

When a couture show focused on everything denim, I wrote that denim was already an American staple and that certain couturiers were copying American cowboys, and their facsimiles everywhere, especially in Harvard Square and at the Widener.

I wrote differently because I was different.

I never forgot where I came from and what I'd become. I'd been an emotionally abused girl who'd contemplated suicide by iodine. I was the girl who had 1,000 invisible angels rotating in a glob that gave me a sense of direction. I was the stockroom girl in danger of molestation.

Now, sitting side-by-side with scions of the fashion industry, I grimaced when designers suggested that women change their look at least four times a day. I harrumphed at the concept of morning clothes being changed for luncheon clothes being changed for cocktail clothes being changed for formals.

Modern women, with or without fluid cash, do not change their clothes four times a day. This was a fake reality. Who has the time? Who has the money? I wrote a daring commentary with an editor's note: if the attached story is too audacious, put it through the shredder, and I'll write something less controversial.

It was teased on the front page.

I wrote that the European couture shows were idea factories for manufacturers of mass-produced clothes. If savvy clothes manufacturers in the audience settled on one look, bought it, toned it down, and made it affordable at a retail level, a relatively small investment could turn into many millions. It was if I'd spilled an open secret. Fashion wasn't only show. Fashion meant business.

I went a giant step further.

Many big-name couturiers, like Chanel and Saint Laurent, had cosmetic lines.

Women who couldn't afford couture clothes, even affordable copies, invested in a new designer lipstick or a designer bottle of cologne. That's how the designers became billionaires. The couture shows were a vehicle that made women everywhere, aware that they could own a designer "something," a cosmetic, and update themselves.

All of my major stories made page one or were teased on page one.

A leading syndicate sold the most controversial columns worldwide. I saw clips of my stories reproduced in many languages. This was not Dumbbell work. Sheila had a significant byline.

A New York City book publisher approached me with a generous contract in hand. Would I write an insider's book about what the European couture world was really like behind the scenes? Would I spill the beans? Speak the truth?

That's the day the book world welcomed me in.

I was twenty-one years old.

That's the day I was really reborn. And Daddy had nothing to do with it.

Epilogue

By the sheer power of her will, and leaning on her fierce imagination, the Dumbbell embarked on a save-yourself journey pioneered in unchartered waters.

That's how she saved herself from hell, from burning, from oblivion.

What she relied on most was her intuition, that true inner voice that tells you what you're thinking and feeling before your brain snaps to attention. She listened hard to what she heard inside. She fabricated her own oasis. She altered her state of being. She thought with her heart.

When the dumbbell pulled 1,000 angels out of thin air, she discovered that their wonderful conversations were between her and herself. That experience was the pivot of her strength, her salvation.

The Dumbbell is a fictitious character, an amalgamation of my own personal experiences blurred into stunning off-the-record vignettes shared with me by thousands of successful people who divulged off-the-record confidences

Marian Christy

about their own bullying.

This happened when I was on a long newspaper interview trail that had nothing whatsoever to do with bullying. I honored these requests. I never printed their names or their stories.

Now, by disguising those decades-old disclosures and weaving them with my own abusive experiences, I've scrambled them into a single camouflaged character. She, who became Sheila, speaks for all those who've been bullied under any circumstance—but especially at home.

M.C.